BERNIE
CLIFTON
CRACKERJACK
TO
VEGAS

BERNIE CLIFTON

CRACKERJACK
TO
VEGAS

MY AUTOBIOGRAPHY

BANNISTER
PUBLICATIONS

First published in Great Britain in 2023 by
Bannister Publications Ltd
Offices 2A, Market Hall, Chesterfield, Derbyshire, S40 1AR
ISBN: 978-1-909813-97-7

Printed and bound in Great Britain by CMP (UK) Ltd

www.bannisterpublications.com

For Stephen

CONTENTS

FOREWORD(S)

BY JIMMY CRICKET, SU POLLARD, JOE PASQUALE, ANITA HARRIS & JOHNNY VEGAS

When a pair of concrete wellingtons the late Sir Ken Dodd gave me for a birthday present were pinched from my garden, I was quite taken aback by the amount of media interest it aroused. A few days after the furore had subsided, I got an email from Bernie. It said - "let me know when you've had enough publicity and I'll bring them back!" How do you describe someone who has the same energy and enthusiasm now that he had when he started off in showbiz? Who is just as funny offstage as he is on? Who ran the London Marathon dressed as an ostrich in the pouring rain to raise money for much-needed causes. Who can have an audience helpless with laughter one minute, then move them to tears when he sings a show-stopping ballad like "Bring Him Home" from the musical "Les Miz" the next? Well, you can describe them in two words - Bernie, Clifton. Buckle-up readers; you're in for a treat!

JIMMY CRICKET

Bernie is so funny he should come with a health warning: **'Heart attack may occur'**. I have known BC for forty years - it seems like four hundred. Nevertheless, he is a consummate performer who brings entertainment and other activities in abundance. He is a terrific wordsmith. Read with pleasure, at your leisure.

SU POLLARD

What can I say about Bernie Clifton that hasn't been said before, something that isn't going to 'spill the beans' and open up a big can of 'whoop-ass' that should never be discussed in the pages of not just this book, but any book? Well, I thought long and hard about it, and in that long and hard time, I realised that Bernie Clifton is an anagram of 'fine nob relict'. Personally, I think that sums up Bernie to 'T'.

He started life in show business as a singer; he was Englebert Humpadink impersonator, but there wasn't a lot of call that in 1938. He was born into a circus family, the son of the bearded lady and the Indian rubber man. When his mother was asked by the midwife when she was in labour did she want a boy or a girl, her reply was that she didn't really care as long as it would fit in the canon. The circus world was not meant for master Clifton. He never made it into any of the shows. The only reason they kept him in the troupe was that he was the only person that could get the tent back in the bag at the end of the week. Instead, he spent his life in the pursuit of making the world laugh. He is, in one word, a 'genius' and another, my friend, Bernie Clifton.

JOE PASQUALE

Hearing the name 'Bernie Clifton' brings the warmth of a smile, a sense of delight and silliness that belies the 'Gentle Man' that is Bernie.

Over the years, we've shared many a 'Bill', like "The Good Old Days", a TV special, or a charity event, and I've treasured them all. But more than ever were the golden moments of "Last Laugh in Vegas". Living in the same mansion with our team of players, watching and admiring Bernie's preparation, his skill and his work ethic and then having a chat over a cuppa' in the middle of the night (without cameras!) He has the kindest heart! All that, and he rescued my knickers! When I put them on the window sill to dry and they blew away in the Sahara wind, landing on top of the umbrellas and palm trees by the swimming pool. What better a friend! What better a feeling than the powerful sense of pride I felt when he got a standing ovation from the Vegas audience for his rendition of 'One Moment in Time" God Bless Bernie Clifton

ANITA HARRIS

Delighted to say a few words about my 'bro', born and bred 'Sentellener'. As a teenager, Bernie actually played on the wing for the Saints B-Team. I was never asked... but I'm not bitter. Eventually, his Ostrich got older (and slower), and I reckon I could take him on the outside if it wasn't for that neck. Let's face it: when it comes to necks, his bird's got the edge.

What a story! From dodging a bomb as a four-year-old to a standing ovation in Las Vegas, it's all here.

Read and enjoy; I know I did."

JOHNNY VEGAS

BEFORE WE START...

JIMMY Tarbuck was in full cry.

One of our most popular comedians was on stage at the Theatre Royal, Nottingham, and went into his 'Tom Jones' routine. As the orchestra played the opening riff to 'It's not Unusual', Jimmy swung the microphone over his head faster and faster in an ever-increasing arc until it was well over the heads of the audience.

Suddenly the microphone head detached itself from the cable and flew, like an Exocet missile, towards the head of a lady in the twelfth row to inflict, surely, a serious injury.

Miraculously, a man in the eleventh row reached up and plucked it out of mid air. The audience gasped, applauded out of sheer relief and a disaster was averted.

To say Jimmy was relieved is a massive understatement, he came offstage shaking and said to yours truly (I was compering that night): "I'll never do that routine again as long as I live, I could have killed that woman".

And that, dear reader, might well have been that – until the mischief genie that has lived with me most of my life popped out of his bottle. "Mmmmm", I thought, "opportunity knocks".

And so, following 24 hours of planning and scheming from myself and members of the stage crew, we arrive the following night at the moment in Jimmy's act where he normally does the 'Tom Jones' routine.

Although having been told earlier by Jimmy: "The Tom Jones bit is out… o….u…t… out", the orchestra started to play "It's not Unusual". Jimmy waved them to stop but they ignored him and continued to play. After several seconds of this, he thought,'what the hell', and swung the microphone round and round over his head at which point the house lights went up and the entire audience bent down and put on hard hats.

Perfect! All the hard work had been worthwhile. Jimmy collapsed, the jape had worked and everyone went home happy.

When I say everyone, there is a long list…

- The stage crew who took me around various building sites borrowing safety helmets.
- The staff at the theatre who kept calling Jimmy to the stage door phone to prevent him overhearing me 'coaching' the audience.
- Johnny Patrick and the Orchestra who refused to stop playing 'It's not Unusual'.
- The technicians who switched on the house lights right on cue.
- The usherettes who distributed the headgear and, lastly, the audience, who willingly and gleefully got involved.

If you're asking "why bother?", there's no ready answer.

But it might help if I take you back to the beginning.

CHAPTER 1
THE EARLY, EARLY DAYS

I was born Bernard Michael Quinn on 22nd April, 1936 – and that's as early as it gets for me. The venue chosen for my arrival was the Peasley Cross Hospital, St Helens, Lancashire. It was convenient for my parents as they lived nearby and didn't have a car, (a car, am I kidding?) So a ten-minute pram push was deemed acceptable.

I was the third son of Daniel and Margaret Quinn, they already had Danny junior and John and within a few years of my entrance came two more boys, Michael and then Anthony… and in the other bed! (stop it and get on with your story)

So there we were, the five Quinn boys, not a sister in sight. I suppose after five, they must have given up.

We grew up at No. 59 Charles Street, opposite the Providence Hospital and right in the middle of a long row of two-bedroomed terraced houses.

A few years later, though, our residential status almost improved to semi-detached, thanks to a developer who came along. What was his name? Yes, Herman Goering, that was him, but I'll come to that little episode in a minute.

It couldn't have been easy for the Quinns, or many of the large families that surrounded us, be they good Catholics or sloppy Protestants. Whatever their religious leanings, life was tough.

So what did they have to lighten up their lives? Well, a few yards down the hill at the bottom of our street was the Theatre Royal, a small variety theatre, where I made my first ever stage appearance. What happened was this...

It was an early Saturday evening in the middle of summer. The brothers Quinn were queuing up for their turn in the tin bath. It had been a blazing hot day, all the doors were open to try and catch whatever breeze there was and through the open doors we could hear the theatre orchestra launch into the overture for the 6.15 performance.

I don't know what came over me – butt naked, except for a little vest that barely reached my waist – but I set off running as fast as my legs could carry me towards the source of the music.

Me Mam gave chase but I was fleet of foot in those days and she was hardly gaining on me. A few seconds later, I made it to the backstage dock doors, left wide open because of the heat. Through the opening, I could see the bright lights and scampered towards them.

I skidded to a halt, centre stage in front of a packed house wearing nothing but that little vest and a cheeky grin. The music died, there was a massive intake of breath from the audience and then, from five hundred throats, came a roar of laughter I shall never forget.

I was in two minds whether to leave the above in...but it proves that this book is definitely NOT a work of fiction.

The events I'll describe actually happened to me. I may have changed a name here and there to avoid any possible offence, but I shall carry on trying to tell it as it was.

So let's get back to Charles Street and that Goering bloke. For the Charles Street residents, September 1941 was a month like any other, there was a war on and danger was everywhere.

As a four year old, I wasn't scared, all I can remember was our sleeping arrangements for which, during the air raid season, the options were as follows:

a) Down the street in Holy Cross Church cellars (they wouldn't dare bomb us there, would they?).
b) Our own back yard in the Anderson Air Raid Shelter, much more fun for a four-year-old!
or c) Under the stairs.

On the night in question, I was bedded down under the stairs with brother John, whilst outside in the shelter with Mam was eight-year-old Danny and, lying snugly in the bottom drawer of a little cupboard, baby Michael, four months to the day.

Dad was on night shift either at the United Glass Bottle Factory or as an Air Raid Warden, perhaps both. So the Quinns, along with the rest of the street, bedded down and tried to get some sleep.

A few doors up at number 69, Vera Cassidy and her family were doing the same. Vera was 14 and used to tease me by making a coin disappear as she moved it from hand to hand. She'd do it again and again and laughed out loud the more mystified I became.

As the night wore on, the children slept while the adults didn't, listening fearfully to the ominous thud of the

3

bombs plastering the Liverpool Docks a few miles down the East Lancs Road.

In years to come, the locals reckoned that, having done their bit in reducing the docks to rubble, the Luftwaffe turned east for home and, on the way, jettisoned whatever was left of their payload.

When 'our' bomb landed, it created a big hole between 63 and 69 and did no good to the neighbouring houses, including ours. I remember everyone screaming and being dragged from under the stairs covered in dust and fallen plaster. Fortunately, our family escaped uninjured and I was too young to appreciate what a close call it had been.

My main memory is of the following morning, walking up our back alley, threading my way through the rubble and passing the spot where the Cassidy's back gate had been. It wasn't there anymore, and tragically neither was Vera. She was gone, at only 14, no more coin tricks on my way to the shop.

I can't say I felt any real sense of grief, though, I assume because I was too young. However, I never stop thinking about the fine line between life and death.

The bomb impacted less than 20 yards from where I was lying, hardly the length of a cricket pitch. Twenty yards, eh, between me and oblivion...20 yards?

Or if you were a bomb aimer, in a Heinkel at 10,000 feet (holding up thumb and finger an inch apart): 'that much'.

Yep, if the plane was flying at, say, 10,000 feet when the bomb was released, I reckon an inch to one side and yours truly, along with the rest of the Quinns, would have been history.

Here's a little poem I wrote about it, many moons ago...

The Ballad of Charles Street

A little lad in Charles Street
Lying in his bed
When a German plane came over and the bomb
*   just missed his head*
It happened 80 years ago
I was four, but still remember… when
The bomb came down on Charles Street
Dark night in September

Back in 1940
They bombed us every night
Down the road in Liverpool
The docks were set alight.
Me dad was in the factory doing night shift
As the bombing raid went on and carried on
He heard the news and set off home
As fast as he could run

And as he turned the corner
Saw the smoke and flames
Headed up to 59
Calling out our names
One by one he pulled us out
Shaken, but alive
Would have been a different story
If we'd lived at 65.

YOUNG LOVE DARES

We often hear that the course of true love never runs smoothly but surely it shouldn't end in humiliation and trauma, especially when it's your 'first time'.

Enter a young lady called Pat Jenkins. She was so pretty that every time she looked at me something happened that previously had only occurred when I'd been playing 'tick rugby' for more than half an hour. I'd get short of breath and my face would go red. She was slim and dark-haired with a fringe that formed a halo over a pair of beautiful large brown eyes, and she had a gorgeous smile. I shall go no further in listing her physical attributes (I was eight years old... there was no 'further').

So there she was, a third-year pupil like me at Holy Cross Junior School, she sat a row ahead and across from me so I could see her profile most of the time. I don't think she ever spoke to me but if she ever caught my eye and smiled, I'd go scarlet and come over all unnecessary.

But there were problems (aren't there always), for she moved in a higher social circle than mine, which was blindingly obvious in one important sartorial area. She had shoes on and I wore clogs.

That's right, clogs! Admittedly, I had socks as well, so I wasn't at the very bottom of the social scale, but not far off.

Looking back, things couldn't have been easy for the Quinns. In 1943 there was still a war on. Everything was rationed and they had five hungry lads to feed. Something had to give and for us it was lino and coconut matting instead of carpets and clogs instead of shoes. The clogs hadn't been a problem for me up till then, as most of the kids on our street wore them.

The best bit about wearing clogs, though, was that

every few weeks we had to go and have new irons fitted. We'd troop down to the 'cloggers' shop at a place in St Helens called 'Fingerpost'. The clogger was a bit like a blacksmith, but with children instead of horses. The difference was that he didn't get kicked or bitten as much, and there was less chance of being shat upon during the course of his work. No, the real difference was that he didn't make us bend our leg up while he gripped it between his knees and nailed the new iron on.

Of course not! That would have been cruel and there was enough cruelty being dished out once they'd got you through the school gates, as I'll tell you in a minute if you'll bear with me.

No, we had to hand over our clogs and sit on a long wooden bench in our socks (those of us that had socks). There weren't many socks that hadn't been darned either but every now and then a dedicated sock watcher could spot a patch so big that it had been knitted prior to being darned to the sock. Aren't you glad, dear reader, that you weren't around and living the St Helens way during the war?

So there we were, clogless, waiting our turn, swinging our unwashed feet in the breeze. Can you imagine the smell? You could cut the air with a clogger's chisel.

So here it is then, the 'best bit': We'd clip clop out of the cloggers with brand new irons on and we'd have a competition to see who could make the most sparks by skidding our feet on the cobbles. It was brilliant and probably the most fun you could have in a week!

(It's all there in the song about the painter, LS Lowry, called 'Matchstick Men': "He painted kids on the corner of the street with their sparking clogs").

No, the main stumbling block to my romance taking off

was geographical. I lived at 59 Charles Street, a stone's throw from the school gates and the lovely Ms Jenkins lived in an area called Moss Bank, a twenty-minute school bus ride away, so there was no way our paths could ever cross outside of school time.

This is where Moira Creevey came in. Moira was in the same class and lived in the next street to me in a terraced house, the front room of which had been turned into a corner shop (as it was in the middle of the terrace it wasn't strictly a 'corner' shop, but you get the picture). Anyway, I used to get my ration of sweets from her mum's shop and one day, as we shared a jelly baby, I started to tell her about my emotional situation. When I got to explaining that my 'plight could never be trothed' because of the distance we lived apart, Moira came up with a brilliant idea.

Why not follow the Jenkins girl home on the school bus and then on to her home? Once I knew exactly where she lived, everything would fall into place.

"Easy!" said Moira and, as a bonus, she would accompany me on my odyssey and give me moral support.

And so the following day after school, instead of taking the short walk to their respective homes, the two young stalkers stood in the bus queue a few furtive places behind their quarry, 'to boldly go where'? Exactly! Where? I'd never been to Moss Bank, didn't know how far it was, how long it would take and hadn't given a thought as to how we would get back…if ever!

A few minutes had passed during which no one had given the two 'aliens' a second glance, so, when the bus arrived, we shuffled forwards with our heads down and clambered upstairs to stay in sight of little Miss J. The bus filled up, the bell rang twice and we were off.

Five minutes later, we were heading out into open

country and hadn't seen a familiar landmark for miles. I looked at Moira, she looked as scared as I did but at least I could see the back of my beloved's head, which helped to quell my fears…and then a raucous voice from behind me.

" TOKENS, PLEASE".

"Moira, what's a token?" (I'd never been on a school bus before and had no idea that a bus token was a metal disc issued to children as a substitute for bus fare).

"TOKENS, COME ON, I HAVEN'T GOT ALL DAY, LET'S HAVE YOUR TOKENS".

We hadn't thought this far ahead, had we? My panic-stricken expression was mirrored by Moira.

Yes, Moira, the architect of this adventure, the person who had convinced me, a lovelorn gormless young boy that nothing could go wrong, that it was okay to follow your loved one to the ends of the earth. Well, alright, if you're going to be picky, only as far as Moss Bank, but that was still a long way when you're little.

"ARE YOU DEAF OR WHAT?"

The conductress snapped her fingers in annoyance and stuck her hand out in front of me. Although by no means old, the hand was wrinkled and dirty, of course it was, it had been handling copper coins and these things called tokens all day.

Do you know, thinking about it, being a clippie on the school run was hardly the best job in the world, was it? I mean I'm not sure what the highlights of a bus crews' job were, (according to Reg Varney it was what went on when his bus was parked by the cemetery gates for a supposed tea break whilst keeping one eye open for Blakey), but I'm sure that collecting bus tokens from a herd of noisy, smelly kids wouldn't be classed as a 'perk'.

"FOR THE LAST TIME, WHERE'S YOUR TOKENS?"

9

"WHAT DO YOU MEAN, YOU HAVEN'T GOT ANY?"

"WHERE DO YOU LIVE?"

"CHARLES STREET?"

"WHAT ARE YOU DOING ON THE SCHOOL BUS IF YOU LIVE IN CHARLES STREET ?"

The bus had fallen silent, but worse than that, Pat Jenkins, without whom I wouldn't have been in this mess, had turned round and was looking straight at me, only this time she wasn't smiling, she was looking at me as if I was a common criminal. My crimson hue deepened. Oh, the shame of it all.

"OFF THE BUS, NOW, THE PAIR OF YOU!"

She rang the bell several times in quick succession and the bus squealed to a halt.

My clogs, feeling heavier than ever, clanked down the metal steps. In happier times, this would have been an opportunity to make good quality sparks, but not now Bernard, not now.

A few moments later, we were standing dejectedly by the side of the road. As the bus pulled slowly away, through the cloud of diesel fumes came her parting shot:

"YOU'LL BE FOR IT IN THE MORNING, MARK MY WORDS. WAIT TILL I TELL SISTER GERTRUDE!"

Oh no, please don't tell Sister Gertrude, I thought as loudly as I could (no point in shouting, the bus was long gone).

Now, however bad I felt about our plight (did I mention we had no idea where we were?) the very mention of Sister Gertrude made it much, much worse.

Sister Gertrude, the headmistress, was a nun (you guessed!) She terrified me and most of the other children who crossed her path. She was tall and gaunt with pinched, severe features, who, on the day she passed out from convent, must have knelt down and asked God: "How may I best serve thee?" and he probably replied, "Go out there and put the fear of ME into those scruffy little buggers* at Holy Cross, especially the ones wearing clogs, verily the footwear of Satan, for do they not maketh sparks with them?"

*Apologies to me Auntie Nora in case she's reading this sitting on a cloud somewhere. I don't intend to demean the Almighty by suggesting he would ever use language like this. I'm just trying to be funny in my own winsome way. And didn't you once say he made us the way we are? So, if you could put me a word in…ta!

So now you've got the picture as we fast forward to the following morning at school assembly in the big hall.

Moira and I had found our way home the night before without resorting to astral navigation. We just kept asking people and an hour or so later we started to recognise signs that we were approaching our own neighbourhood: small things like broken windows, bloodstained pavements and cats with cauliflower ears.

We had also avoided problems in our respective households by fibbing that we had been at each others houses listening to an omnibus edition of 'Dick Barton Special Agent' (don't ask! You had to be there!). We also felt better when we realised our school bus 'bailiff' hadn't taken our names and convinced ourselves we'd got off lightly.

So, as we filed into the hall along with almost 200 other pupils, we had no reason to dwell on the trauma of the previous evening and in an attempt to purge the event from my mind, I was even managing to avoid catching the eye of Mrs Jenkins' daughter.

It was a familiar scene, repeated daily. A few hundred of us standing in class groups waiting for the ritual prayers and hymns to start, with the teachers attempting to keep us in tune and in time.

And here they come, in single file, led by Miss Wilson who made her way to the piano, followed by Sister Margaret (very pleasant, obviously missed out on the 'God' chat), then Mrs Shacklady, a lovely 'mumsy' teacher (see, they weren't all bad), and then the rearguard, Mrs Fairhurst (fearsome woman, more of her anon) and finally Sister Gertrude herself, along with A BUS CONDUCTRESS!

Why would a bus conductress be standing up there with all the teachers for morning assembly?

Perhaps it was going to be a wartime equivalent of the Susan Boyle 'Britain's got Talent' moment. We would all start singing 'Ave, Ave, Ave Maria', then she would step forward, unbuckle her ticket machine and in a beautiful soprano voice take the last chorus solo. She would finish to thunderous applause from all present and a Star is Born. (In your dreams, Bernard, in your dreams!).

"QUIET, ALL OF YOU, QUIET!"

A deathly hush fell on the whole school, marred only by the footsteps of the headmistress and the conductress walking slowly down the middle aisle looking intently right and left as they travelled and the sound of a steam hammer crashing out an ear-piercing rhythm in my chest!

Almost 70 years have passed since the incident, a whole lifetime, yet I can still remember the feeling, the same cold hand of fear gripping me as if it were yesterday. Moira was spotted first, she was a row ahead of me.

"THATS ONE OF 'EM!"

"AHA! MOIRA CREEVY"

"TAKE HER OUT AND SHOOT HER!" (I exaggerate).

Now it was my turn. I was not too difficult to spot, as the heat from my crimson face was fetching off the flowered wallpaper. If blushing had been an Olympic Event, I'd have been a young legend.

"AND THAT'S THE OTHER ONE"

"BERNARD QUINN AND MOIRA CREEVY, MY OFFICE, NOW!"

All they had to do now was to punish us in some way.

What do you reckon? We were a bit young for caning, (they'd make up for that later), so the options might be:

- a) Extra homework.
- b) Detention.
- c) 100 lines: 'I must not board the school bus without a token'.

No! None of those: too simple!

They needed to heap something else upon us.

A word I used in the opening sentence of this chapter: humiliation!

Every afternoon, there was a kind of crèche in the school hall where mums could leave their three and four year olds for a spot of lunch, a bit of playtime and then a snooze for an hour lying on fold-up camp beds.

On the premise that; 'If you want to behave like children, you're going to be treated like children', we were taken from our classroom after lunch that day and made to lie down with the 'babies' for their siesta.

What was wrong with these people? How sick was that?

Anyway, after about an hour of lying down with my

eyes tightly shut I heard their footsteps coming round the beds.

"Right, Moira, go back to your class and behave yourself in future"

Then to my bed, "Right, Bernard", (the bed was kicked, but I was having none of it. I was feigning sleep).

"BERNARD", (No way! I was asleep wasn't I? If they wanted me to sleep with the babies that's what I would do. Like a hardened criminal, I would do my 'time').

I know...pathetic!

Hilarity from above.

"Oh, lets leave him then"

Five minutes later, another kick at the bed.

"BERNARD QUINN" (No way was I giving in).

Hoots of laughter from the staff. I was making their day.

"Isn't it amazing, he's fast asleep yet he's blushing".

(Remember? I was good at blushing).

"BERNARD QUINN!"

This time the bed was kicked so hard I almost fell out, so reluctantly I 'woke up'.

"BACK TO YOUR CLASS... NOW".

And off I slouched, scarred mentally for life. Well, that's been my excuse for the way I've behaved from that moment on.

And what of my romance with Pat Jenkins? It died a natural death, I'm afraid. Drowned in the trauma. I was never the same lad from that day forward. I don't want to be too dramatic but it has made me wonder how much 'baggage' we hide and how harmful it might be for us.

Read on for more 'baggage' news...

BOWED BUT UNBROKEN

Yes, there's more to come from my time at Holy Cross, so let's deal with the worst first.

My first contact with Mrs Fairhurst was, how shall I put it, very violent...no, it's got to be the other way round: Mrs Fairhurst's first contact with me was very violent...that's more like it!

I had now moved up to my penultimate year in Mrs Shacklady's Class, a whole year before the 'Fairhurst War of Attrition' began.

I liked Mrs Shacklady but, more importantly, I'm certain Mrs Shacklady liked children, a quality you might have thought was essential in a primary school teacher but one, as you've gathered, that wasn't shared by some of her colleagues.

Despite spending a whole year in her class there's only one thing I can remember: one morning she came in looking unusually severe and asked for our attention before lessons began.

"Boys and girls, I must say how upset I was this morning as I walked through the streets where many of you live."

That's true, half the school lived within half a mile of the main gates, but what's she getting at?

"Most of your front steps had empty milk bottles on them and I was appalled to see that the majority of those empty bottles had not been rinsed out".

What heinous crime is this? Don't tell Sister Gertrude, she'll have our parents killed! Please don't tell her, even if it means missing out on the orphanage trip to Southport on Easter Monday!

"So, boys and girls, even if your parents are too busy to

do it themselves, please make sure that all your empty milk bottles are rinsed out before they are put on the front step."

And that's it, one whole year in her class and that's the only thing I can remember from it.

One day, the whole school was marched down to the Parish Church to rehearse some kind of religious festival or other, I'm not sure what it was. The classes were entering the Church in order of age, youngest first, so our class, with me towards the rear, was queuing outside, which is when I started mucking about as there was no sign of Mrs Shacklady who had gone on ahead, so I had a clear field, or so I thought.

I hadn't realised that the final year class had turned up behind us, led by the Fairhurst Ogre. I can't remember exactly what I was doing to make my friends laugh, only that it involved some kind of lunatic dance, when...BAM! BAM!

I was knocked off my feet and, yes, as I was in mid air, I actually wet my pants!

It was the Fairhurst person, doing her impression of Mrs Vlad the Impaler. She then dragged me upright and shook me like a rag doll while bellowing something about "sacrilege".

"We're outside the church, does it still count as sacrilege?" I asked .

I'm joking, of course, I was too busy counting my teeth and wondering how long it would be before my wet pants started to smell like our cat's litter tray.

Anyway, the point is I was being naughty and deserved disciplining, but this kind of assault? I don't think so.

As you can imagine, having got off to a bad start with Mrs F, I wasn't looking forward to my final year under her savagery, sorry, tutelage. A year which ended with the sitting of the 11-plus exams, success in which meant a Grammar School place.

It wasn't a happy time for me and for most of my classmates, as she was on our backs all of the time. I'm sure we deserved some of it, but when you're under the cosh the whole time, you become cowed.

It became clear, that Mrs Fairhurst's skills, apart from having a black belt in G.B.H. against minors, didn't include morale boosting of under-12s, when, just before the exams, she said to me: "Bernard Quinn, the day you pass your 11-plus, little pigs will fly"

Unbelievably, a few weeks later when the results came out, I'd only bloody passed, hadn't I? Incredible!

I thought there must have been a mix-up at first but, no, it was official, I'd passed.

First chance I got, I marched straight up to her, waved my pass certificate under her horrible nose, pointed up at the sky and shouted "Look Mrs Fairhurst, a pig, and it's flying". (Of course I didn't, she would have beaten me to a pulp, but many's the time I wish I had).

Well, happily I can say, that's almost the end of my Junior School story, apart from the fact that my wearing clogs came back to bite me. A few weeks before I left, a former pupil who had passed the 11-plus the year before came to see us to prepare us for what lay ahead. He took one look at me and said: "You won't be going to t'Grammar School wearing those".

"What do you mean?" I asked.

"It's t'Grammar School you clot, they won't let you in wearing clogs, nobody wears clogs at t'Grammar School".

It's hard to say what a smack in the face that was for me. I've never forgotten how it made me feel. I took off, walked out of the school and trudged round the fields crying my eyes out until I finally went back in.

I met Mrs Shacklady, who saw that I was upset and when I explained, told me not to worry, everything would be fine.

And it was. I don't how, whether she had a word with my Mam and Dad or whether they scrimped a bit harder, but a few weeks later, towards the end of the summer holidays, I got a new pair of shoes and said goodbye to the clogs for ever and, do you know, I didn't miss the sparks, not at the time anyway.

Looking back over this period of my school life, it seems to have been largely unhappy and traumatic. I'm sure there were many happy times, too, but it's significant that I don't recall them.

So I couldn't wait to move up to grammar school, but as I was to discover, there would be many times when I would long to be back in the Juniors...clogs and all!

CHAPTER 2
FROM A SMACK TO A THRASH

I was one of the last to enter Lower 3B classroom that September morning in 1947. Most of the desks had been occupied, but there were still one or two not taken.

I hovered in the doorway, fit for a juvenile catwalk in my new West Park green blazer, grey shirt with matching striped tie, regulation grey short trousers, long grey socks (brand new: no patches) and, wait for it, brand new black lace-up shoes, all of which had been bought over the summer with money my folks hadn't got. My eyes scanned back and forth looking desperately for a friendly face, for there were several of us who had graduated from Holy Cross. Then my name was called… twice. There, in the front row, right under the rostrum that would be manned by the teacher was Billy Forshaw, with an empty chair beside him.

And there in the very back row, in the far corner, at the furthest possible point in the room from any supervision was Tommy Anderton, again with an empty chair beside him.

I knew both Billy and Tommy very well, we'd been classmates for the last four years. Billy was red haired, freckled and clever. Tommy was pudgy and, er, like me, not so clever.

Both lads had called to me in unison: "Bernard, sit here!", motioning to the empty chair beside them.

So, I'd been in Higher Education for five minutes and already I was called upon to make a decision.

My options: to sit in the front row under the nose of the teacher, next to a clever lad who would work hard and be successful; or, to sit in the back row, almost out of sight of authority, next to a lad who, to put it kindly, was likely to avoid work at all costs and get in all sorts of trouble.

I made my choice and seconds later. "Ta, Billy", I said as I hung my satchel over the back of my chair and sat down next to him. NO, OF COURSE I DIDN'T!

Own up! There isn't one person reading this who'd have said I'd sit next to Billy Forshaw. If I had joined him, I think I'd be writing a vastly different story.

Of course, it was a no brainer. I hurried over to the back corner of the class, sat next to Tommy and felt better already… for about twelve seconds.

"QUIET, YOU LOT!"

The command was obeyed instantly by all 30 of us.

It came from a man, which was a novelty, all our teachers in the lower School were women, so my fear factor this particular morning was raised considerably. The fact that he was dressed in similar fashion to a priest didn't help either.

West Park Grammar was staffed by a religious teaching order, the De La Salle Brothers along with a few civilian teachers, mainly men, with only a couple of women on board, (any hopes I may have harboured that there might be a 'soft touch' amongst the latter variety were soon shattered, as I was to discover sooner rather than later).

I didn't know back then that I was to fail miserably as a student. Neither did me Mam and Dad, otherwise they would never have lashed out on the School uniform. The trouble was I never got up to speed with the information I was being asked to absorb on a daily basis.

I didn't get any of it. Not the Chemistry, the Physics, the French, and as for the Maths, well, don't even go there.

I was non-academic, someone who, through no fault of his own, had 'fluked' his 11-plus and, therefore, was due to spend the next four years being punished for his failings by a few outwardly respectably professionals with psychopathic tendencies. Gosh, I'm glad I got that out of my system. That was very therapeutic!!

GOODWILL TO ALL MEN (AND BOYS?)

Christmas Day 1947 had got off to a good start.

Up early, opened the presents, porridge for breakfast, down the street to 10 o'clock Mass, back home for a few hours assembling the Meccano (long before Lego had been thought of) and, after lunch, back to the Meccano on the big table in the kitchen.

The whole family was there, boys with their toys and Mam and Dad sitting round the fire enjoying a sherry with my Uncle John, who suddenly mentioned cousin Colin, same age and a fellow pupil at West Park but in a different class to me, lower 4A.

"Colin did well in't first term, came fourth in t'class, eck of a good report he got".

The sweet smell of Christmas vanished to be replaced by the familiar stench of fear

"Report?" questioned me Dad.

My fingers fumbled with the nuts and bolts in front of me as my whole Christmas began to fall apart.

"Report?".

My colour started to rise and I found it hard to breathe.

"Did you get a report, Bernard ?".

"Yes".

"Where is it?"

"In the parlour."

My report was so bad I'd been unable to pluck up the courage to show it to them. As I was the first of their brood to reach grammar school, they didn't know that at the end of each term a 'report' was compiled by the teachers, then given to the pupil to be handed on to the parents to be signed and returned.

Let's face it, I wasn't best placed to get them up to speed with the procedure, was I?

"Go and fetch it".

The room fell silent apart from the sound of my embarrassed Uncle John tapping out his pipe on the fireguard. The Angel on the Tree in the corner bowed her head in shame as I returned and handed over my death warrant. The document had been burning a hole in my blazer pocket for more than a week.

"Twenty ninth, twenty ninth?"

Was it really necessary to repeat it, surely the whole street knew by now.

"How many's in the class ?"

"Er, thirty one".

I wondered if Maurice Greenwood and James Farrington were suffering a similar or even worse trauma: "thirty first?".

(I can't remember which way round it was, I only know I didn't come last).

Hey, Maurice and James, if you're out there, please don't sue me for the naming and shaming. I'm just telling it as I remember it. I'm sure you've survived your Grammar School traumas better than I have.

Anyway, my Christmas day was ruined and it can't have been much fun for Uncle John either; he only popped in for a dram and looked what happened, he morphed into some kind of pipe smoking 'Bad Santa'.

THE PAIN GOES ON

My enduring memories of grammar school are unhappy ones, as you may have gathered.

I was actually given the captaincy of the school's 2nd cricket team (I was good at something, then) but it was just a brief respite from the fear and pain arising from regular academic failures and subsequent (physical) punishment.

The pattern was soon established. I was never able to grasp the basics of most of the subjects and as a result, was being caned on an almost daily basis.

'Spare the rod and spoil the child' was a popular saying of the time and 'six of the best' another, which meant three strokes on each hand with a bamboo cane.

Fellow pupil Anthony Harrison had lost a finger in an accident so was given only four strokes on his good hand (I'm not making this up). Who came up with that? Did they vote on it during a coffee break? Why four strokes and not three, or even five? There must have been an edict from up high because it was the same from each and every teacher.

Teachers had different methods. One would strike

only the very tips of your fingers, even if it meant missing a few times, so that your fingertips would be black and blue for hours. Another used a length of three-inch wide rubberised belt which meant the whole of your palm became swollen. The pain was unbearable, we would scuttle back to our seats, holding back the tears and sitting on our hands, every now and then there'd be an audible sob from a lad with a low pain threshold but, for the most part, we suffered in silence.

In spite of the daily beatings, I don't think we became cowed, after all it was the same for everybody and you wouldn't even think about showing your battle scars to your parents. Let's face it, there was always a half chance of a good hiding when you got home for some domestic misdemeanour or other.

It was the culture of the time. Our teachers and parents were hitting us because they too had been hit. It's just the way it was.

I found that music helped me to forget the pain, if only for a short time. I used to get fourpence a day to cover my return bus fare and I began to walk home, saving tuppence. On my route was a grubby 'egg and chips' cafe with a juke box. I would walk in, put two pennies in the slot and stand motionless in front of the machine for three minutes whilst it blared out my choice, which was always 'Buttons and Bows' by Dina Shore.

To this day, I'm word perfect on the lyrics: "My bones denounce the buckboard bounce and the cactus hurts my toes, let's go where the girls keep wearing those silks and satins and linen that shows and I'm all yours in buttons and bows".

I loved it then and still do today.

Then, as soon as the song ended, I would turn round and walk out.

Strange behaviour for a twelve-year-old but I was a miserable little sod and it seemed to help.

I could lose myself in the song if only for a couple of minutes.

MY FIRST (SECOND-HAND) MAKEOVER

Peer pressure is never very far away when you're thirteen. It was the way Arthur Cunningham dressed that was my concern. As if being a national amateur boxing champion wasn't enough, Arthur was always very smart.

It worried me Mam that we even knocked around together. Having discovered that he already had a girl friend she memorably described him as being 'old headed'.

In contrast, I was anything but. She worked very hard at keeping a very young head on my shoulders, and heaven forbid I should even look at a girl, never mind go out with one. It didn't help that I was very scruffy.

The Quinns didn't have a clothes budget. I've already told you what it took to get me out of clogs and into shoes but even so it was clear I needed a new top coat, winter was approaching and gabardine 'Macs' were all the rage.

So one afternoon, me and Mater took the trolley bus, not to a teenage fashion show but to Moira Brown's house. Moira lived with her Mum and Dad in a terraced house but, unlike ours, it was smart and the family may well have been middle class. They really did have fruit on the sideboard when nobody was ill; I was so impressed when I saw some, let me tell you.

The reason for the trip was laid out on the sofa.

A light brown gabardine Mackintosh – wow!

Look out, Arthur, I could be a threat.

I didn't need much bidding to try it on and it fitted a treat. It wasn't new but that didn't bother me. I knew that, wearing this, I would hold my own on the West Park catwalk.

I also had problems fastening the buttons, needing maternal help to complete the task, but I had supposed that was because it was double breasted.

Tell you what, though, as we returned home I looked in every shop window to catch the reflection of the new teenage fashion icon formerly known as Bernard Quinn.

I had no interest in the history of the garment. Okay it was second hand, a slight stigma, but who would know? It's provenance was of no concern to me, until... Monday morning came and I was setting off to wear it for school. I was still struggling with the fastening when it dawned on me why it was proving so difficult.

The buttons were on the wrong side: IT WAS A GIRL'S MAC!

Oh no, I WAS WEARING MOIRA BROWN'S OLD MAC!

Here I was, almost fourteen, becoming aware of the first rumblings of adolescence on a daily (perhaps nightly) basis; an avid reader of well-thumbed copies of 'Health and Efficiency', the nudist magazine; and familiar with the racier chapters from the pen of a certain Hank Jansen and I was wearing a Girl's Mac.

My face turned crimson and I began to panic. In tears, I confronted Mother.

"Who'll know?", she asked.

"Well, I will for a start, and suppose Arthur Cunningham finds out, I'll be the laughing stock of 4B."

"Well, it's all we can afford, it's Moira Brown's mac or nothing".

I trudged off to school with heavy heart. It didn't help that I got some compliments from my classmates. I was wearing a badge of shame and they hadn't spotted it yet. When Arthur was advising me how to wear it in a snappier way by gathering the spare material to the sides and showing a crease-free front, I was convinced I'd be exposed.

But do you know, he never noticed nor did anyone else?

I wore it for some time but only during bad weather and never with ease and was more than happy to hand it down to my younger brother Michael when the time came.

I wonder how he handled it.

Do you think we're affected later in life by this kind of childhood situation?

I don't know, but the fact that I can remember every nuance of that mac 60 years later must be significant.

CHAPTER 3
BRING ON THE BREAD

It was blindingly obvious that my school days were numbered.

I had tried to alleviate my parents' suffering by altering my school reports using an ink rubber, and perhaps changing 30% to 80% for instance. Pathetic, I know, but that's how desperate I was. But inevitably the end was in sight.

After a set of calamitous exam results topped by the following: Arithmetic: Nil; Algebra: Nil; Geometry: Nil; (surely some kind of record); my parents were called in and it was agreed I would leave at the age of 15.

I didn't even take the forthcoming exams, no point. A couple of weeks before the school year ended, I slunk out of West Park for the last time.

No goodbyes or fond farewells. Oh, the ignominy!

That was a Friday and the following Monday morning, I was summoned to the local Co-op grocery store to join the world of retail.

What happened to my 'gap year', I hear you cry!

No flies on Mrs Quinn. "If he can't learn, he'll have to earn," was her motto.

So having left the world of education with head bowed, what would I make of my debut as a working lad?

The bottom rung on the grocery ladder was the one occupied by a callow youth, a heavy basket full of loaves and an even heavier bicycle. I was given a grubby notebook with the bread delivery details and then shown the 'bike'. It was the type with a tiny front wheel and a huge basket on the front.

That's right, I was the original 'Hovis' boy.

With a full basket, this machine was impossible for me to ride, the centre of gravity being way too high, so I had to push it until the load was reduced.

Then something happened that first morning. I remember it as if it were yesterday.

I was standing at a street junction waiting to push the bike across the main road, when the West Park school bus crawled past and there, on the lower deck just a few feet away, was my former classmate Christopher Boydell.

His expression when he saw me was memorable.

It was a classic moment. The gaze was held for a few seconds without any normal signs of recognition being exchanged. For his part, he was totally nonplussed, being unable to understand the scenario.

"Classmate on Friday? Bread lad on Monday ?"

As for me, it was blindingly clear in which direction I was heading.

Three days earlier, there I was, blazered and flannelled, part of a prestigious centre of learning, and now? I'm working at the Co-op, delivering bread. Oh, calamity!

It wasn't easy for me being a bread lad. For a start, I kept losing track of what bread should go where. I could hardly tell a small 'brown' from a medium 'white', plus I had to keep my head down every time a school bus went past.

I was out in all weathers and always struggling to keep that bike from toppling over.

Things went from bad to worse: the monsoon was in full spate as I trundled the fully-laden behemoth down College Street. I completely lost control, the bike started to fall over and even though I caught a few, the bulk of the load of (unwrapped) loaves cascaded all over the wet pavement and came to rest in the gutter.

At this point, not even a master baker could have separated the brown from the white.

There I was, on hands and knees, wiping the mud off the bread with the aid of a very grubby hanky in order to complete my delivery round. Can you imagine the health and safety issues?

But for how much longer would the local population survive my delivery methods? According to the minutes of the hastily-arranged meeting between the shop manager and my career consultant, one Margaret Quinn, the answer was, 'not very'.

"You'll be far better off with a 'trade'," she said.

Of course, a trade!

Delivering bread would never lead to a trade, not even with a spot of 'Loaf Juggling' thrown in.

Mrs Q held the view that a 'trade' was essential for my future welfare. She also had it figured that if the family home was full of tradesmen, all the odd jobs that needed doing would be carried out with expertise – on the cheap!

That's why eldest son Danny was already an apprentice carpenter, next son John an engineer, so naturally Bernard would have to be an… electrician.

It didn't matter that I might not have a talent for the job, that wasn't an issue.

So I was marched round to Rothery's, the local TV, radio and electrical store, had an interview and was set on, not initially as an apprentice electrician but as a 'trainee TV aerial erector'.

Wouldn't that mean climbing ladders and crawling round on people's roofs? Had anyone bothered to ask if I had a head for heights?

Mrs Quinn, is that your Bernard up here, he looks frightened. He is frightened!

The idea was that I would prove myself as a useful member of the workforce and then be promoted to become an apprentice 'sparky'.

It appeared to work. Within a few weeks I was at ground level. Either I'd displayed a real talent at roof height or the boss had seen me in action and said "get him down before the little bugger falls off".

I had a few weeks of mainly helping with rewiring industrial premises, shoving cables under floorboards and listening to the rats retreating. It was not the work environment I would have chosen, but I wasn't in a position to complain.

But that weekend I learned a new word. Our boss, Mr Jacques, picked us up from a job in Liverpool one Saturday lunchtime and invited me to join him in the cab of the pick-up instead of sitting in the back with the other lads. I thought that was nice of him, especially as it became apparent he wanted to extend my vocabulary.

The new word he taught me was 'aptitude'.

I didn't know what it meant but he made it clear it was something I hadn't got or, if I had, not enough of it to remain a member of the Rothery Radio team of skilled artisans.

He seemed really sorry that I didn't have this 'aptitude' thing. As for me, I wasn't that bothered, especially when I worked out that without it I'd be having a lie-in come Monday.

Mrs Quinn had other ideas! She claimed that there had never been a layabout in the history of the Quinn dynasty and vowed her third son wouldn't be the first.

Now no one could dispute the fact that my initial attempts at dipping my toe into the pond of employment had ended badly.

The first one had come to grief following a swathe of letters from numerous customers of the St Helens Co-operative Society asking: "Could we please have a little more bread with our next delivery of mud?" The second was simply down to an unexpected attack of aptitude deficiency.

So where next for this struggling offspring?

PLUMB CRAZY

Time to seek help from a higher power!

So off they trotted, mother leading, son trailing, not to church, but to the headquarters of the St Helens Corporation Building Department.

Just to put you straight on the use of the term 'higher power'. The chances of getting a job at the 'Corp' were greatly enhanced if you were a Catholic.

Even better if you were seen taking Holy Communion at the same church attended by the depot boss, a Mr Thomas Caulfield.

Which is why mother and child were quickly ushered in to the main man's office.

Once the 'communion' criteria had been established and I was seen to be sound in wind and limb, we were back out on the street, Mrs Q wearing a satisfied smile and the boy Bernard wondering if he should mention that he really didn't want to spend the rest of his life being a plumber.

It would make no difference. The die was cast. Hallelulah! I had a trade.

Within hours I had been kitted out with bib and brace overalls and found myself on a building site reporting to the foreman plumber, Mr Tom Fitzgerald.

A Catholic? What do you think?

I was given the job of 'can lad', which involved going round the site collecting all the enamel tea cans belonging to the workmen and making sure they were all full of hot tea made in a large gas boiler when the tea break whistle went at 10 o'clock, same again at noon and at three o'clock.

Woe betide you if the water wasn't boiling five minutes before break time. To deprive the British worker of his tea on the dot was simply unacceptable.

My duties also involved running errands for different tradesmen and this is when I first became a victim of the practical jokes aimed at new arrivals.

For instance, I'd be sent down to the store room to ask for some 'striped' paint or perhaps a 'new bubble' for a spirit level and so on until I was promoted to go 'on the tools' and hand over the 'cans' to a younger, unfortunate lad.

This 'joke' culture was very prominent on the site. It was a way to find some relief from the daily grind.

Everybody was at it and I needed no encouragement to 'get on board'.

Some of the jokes were quite cruel. There was a gas fitter, Jack Topping, who used to commute from Liverpool every day, a round trip of over twenty miles. By push bike!

His trusty steed was a real 'sit up and beg' model and he needed legs of steel to propel it.

He could have come on the bus and was given a daily allowance to cover the fare, but chose to pocket the money and cycle instead.

It was decided to raise his fitness levels. Each day when he was out on the site 'fitting gas', his bike would be worked on without his knowledge. The idea was to make it heavier a little at a time. The handlegrips were taken off, rolls of lead inserted in the handlebars and the grips replaced. A few days later, a similar operation which meant removing the seat was carried out. Then the saddlebags were dismantled, lined with sheet lead and re-assembled.

After a few weeks, he used to arrive unfit to work and was persuaded to use his travel allowance to buy a motor bike.

A few more examples: a cardboard box left in the middle of the road inviting someone to come along and kick it. There'd be a brick inside!

An enamel mug would have a tiny hole drilled under the lip at right angles to the handle causing the drinker to constantly dribble his tea.

You'd be looking for your bike at knocking off time and there it was, on a roof, roped to a chimney with all ladders hidden out of sight.

Young apprentices would be held down, spread eagled

on an upper floor scaffold, their clothing nailed to the boards and left unable to move.

It was a constant, there was always something going on.

During the winter, the site soon became a swamp and often the only way to negotiate the distance between adjacent houses was by a walkway of planks placed on bricks, a perilous journey, the danger heightened by the possibility that loitering by an upstairs window might be a youth with mischief on his mind.

The idea was to wait until the victim was halfway across and then launch a series of large missiles, house bricks and the like, these would be aimed at the swamp adjacent to the plank. We would award ourselves points depending on the amount of mud the target would be spattered in.

It's amazing the amount of time we'd spend waiting for a victim. Following a heavy rainfall, we'd lurk up there for hours at a time, and the choice of 'missile' was crucial. A chunk of paving stone was ideal but not too heavy, otherwise it might affect the accuracy of the throw, too light and the mud 'wave' wouldn't be enough. A piece around a foot square was thought to be ideal.

I reckon if I'd been born a few years earlier, I might have been special adviser to Barnes Wallis!

"Ah, Bernard, thanks for popping in, I know you're busy, but I need your help with this Dambusting raid. I'm not sure what type of bomb to use, any ideas?"

"Paving Stones? Brilliant! Why didn't I think of that?"

But there was other stuff to learn: I found out that the way to determine the length of a coil of lead pipe was to measure the radius and then multiply by three and a bit. That's a fact! Summat called 'pies are square'!

Then there was... the co-efficient of linear expansion!

It's where different materials, when heated, expand at different rates.

So if you couldn't get the lid off a jar of jam, you held it in very hot water for thirty seconds and then the top would walk off because the metal lid had expanded faster than the glass. Please don't try this at home!

More useful knowledge was gained at night school.

For instance... gravity and how to defy it!

Let's say an apprentice plumber, sitting on a high stool, was occupied in lead burning, the method of joining two sheets of lead together using an acetylene torch.

It's a process that requires intense concentration and should be carried out in total silence.

Now, if two fellow apprentices were to creep up and stand on a bench just behind him, carrying between them a large sheet of steel plate which they then dropped onto the concrete floor, it's absolutely certain that the lead-burning person would contradict the laws of gravity and rise into the air. Daylight would actually appear between the stool and the seat of the poor boy's pants.

Be honest, of the last three examples shown, the last one is a stand-out winner and, as a bonus, the repertoire of obscenities held by anyone within earshot would increase tenfold.

However, this kind of activity could be very tiring and a lad needed to unwind whenever possible at the end of a working week. One way of relaxing was to go to t'pictures...

TEN O CLOCK RALLY

I was just one of a motley crew of youths who shuffled into the Rivoli Cinema that Sunday evening... but we weren't there to watch the films.

In the mid 1950s, Sunday cinema had just started. Prior to that, entertainment on the Sabbath was banned and there was really nowhere for us to go. Then the government overcame the objections of the Lord's Day Observance Society and allowed the cinemas to open.

So, in common with many other provincial towns, the entire teenage population headed for the 'pictures'.

It was the place to be, there were girls there, of course, but, more importantly for our lot, there was an opportunity for mischief.

On a good night we'd muster up to twenty strong. Amongst us there'd be the Sweeney brothers, Bernard and Denis, Jimmy Martindale, Terry O'Connor, Johnny Duffy, 'Moggy' and 'Ged' Moore, Johnny Fitzgerald, Gordon Spencer and Bernard Quinn (that's me, folks).

The films being shown were, to be kind, extremely average. The Sunday fare being served up consisted of elderly black-and-white British 'B' movies supporting early American technicolour 'epics' that didn't make it first time around.

So unsurprisingly, the audience reaction to these offerings, was in the main, derisory. Lots of heckling went on and as we were sitting in the dark, most of it vulgar. The irony being that most of the above named had attended Mass earlier in the day.

The highlight of the evening had nothing to do with the action on screen. When the hands on the cinema clock approached ten o'clock an expectant hush fell over the assembled throng.

Furtively, in the seconds leading up to the hour, various items were being produced from pockets… mouth organs, bicycle bells, bird calls, motor horns, etc.

And then, through the darkness, came the cry… "TEN O CLOCK RALLY".

The cacophony of noise that erupted drowned out the sound track of the film (as if anyone cared), and was greeted with a roar or approval by the rest of the audience.

Chaos ensued, the house lights came on, with staff running down the aisles to the source of the din, suspects were hauled out and searched, but nothing was ever found, the evidence had already been passed along the line to a 'safe' area.

What was going on then? Just a slice of wonderful nonsense.

I'd wondered if something similar was going on in cinemas elsewhere and thanks to some informal research carried out by a local friend, 'rallyer' Tommy Bracken, it would appear not.

Tommy remembers being involved at another local cinema, the Thatto Heath Empire, and has evidence of further 'episodes' at two cinemas in Prescot a couple of miles further out, but enquiries in neighbouring towns drew a blank.

I do wonder why this particular piece of nonsense seemed peculiar to St Helens and nowhere else.

The nights out with the lads were great fun, but there was something else going on in my life. You see I was a singer !

Yes, I could sing and, if I say so myself, my vocalising sounded good in the venues I'd appeared in (various bathrooms on the building site). The acoustics enhanced the vocals brilliantly and I began to dream about becoming Britain's answer to Eddie Fisher.

Most of the local pubs had a singing room with a pianist where you could get up and chance your arm (the later the hour the more numerous the singers), but I wanted to sing with a band and that would have to be at the local dance hall, the 'Co-op'.

Or to give it the full title, the St Helens Co-operative Society Ballroom.

The ballroom was in the Helena House building, on the top floor above the grocery shop where a few years earlier I'd set up my mud delivery business.

So I had history at the Co-op.

Oh, yes, and there's something else you should know: I was officially banned from the ballroom!

The 'enforcer' was the manager, Sylvester Burrows.

What happened was this. A few weeks earlier, our Saturday night revelling had 'peaked' at the Co-op. We rolled in after the pubs closed, at the last possible moment. We were worse for drink, as were most of the lads at the dance. But unlike them, we weren't looking for girls, we were looking for mischief.

For instance, we would watch a staff member enter the walk-in cupboard under the balcony to restock the kiosk with cigarettes, then we'd slam the door behind him and lock it! The band would be playing loudly, but now they had an extra percussionist as the poor man banged on the door to be let out.

On the night of the ban, we excelled ourselves. Along with my accomplice, Gordon Spencer, I'd smuggled in a length of bamboo curtain rod. I took my shirt off and tied it round my neck like a cape, then hijacked the doormens' bikes and radically altered the mood of a slow foxtrot by invading the floor with our very own jousting tournament.

A Knight on a Bike with a Curtain Rod as a Lance.

The effect was dramatic. The dancers stopped dancing and formed two lines cheering on their favourite knight. It was lunacy!

The band played on but were completely ignored, the dancers focusing on our ridiculous joust.

The hilarity was short lived. I was frogmarched into the gents' toilets by the bouncers to be confronted by an incandescent Mr Burrows, who accused me of attempting to ruin his business.

Gordon reminded me recently of some of the exchanges...

ME (slurred), " What's up Mr Burrss."

Mr B (apoplectic) "You're an Imbecile."

GORDON (peacemaker) "He's alright really."

Mr B (on fire) "Alright? He's got no bloody shirt on"

I was then thrown out and told "YOU'RE BANNED".

A couple of weeks later, I'd started to creep into the ballroom again but, so far, had avoided being seen by Mr B.

I then heard that the band's vocalist, Brian Heaney, a great singer who I'd envied for years, was leaving due to National Service and I saw my chance.

The following Monday evening, in the almost empty hall, I wandered up to the bandstand and, only slightly the worse for wear, asked Bert Webb the bandleader for an audition.

He looked down at me from the sharp end of his saxophone,

"So you're a singer, are you ? "

I said I was.

"Friday, half past seven, in a suit... sober ".

The reference to dress code was because at the time I was wearing sports coat and flannels, alright for a Monday but not suitable for a band singer. Ever!

I had my song ready, a big hit at the time entitled 'Love is a Many Splendoured Thing'. I'd often heard Brian sing it, so was familiar with the arrangement.

I got round the suit criteria by 'borrowing' my big brother's brown pin stripe. Not so much Armani, more like 'Ar Danny's'.

Friday evening, a quarter to eight and to a deserted ballroom, the suit made it's debut.

As I finished the song (to absolute silence), Bert looked over his shoulder towards me,

"Not bad!"

Over an interval cup of tea, he told me I'd got the job, provided I turned up four nights a week and learned the repertoire for a waltz, quickstep, foxtrot and tango.

Then he went into Mr Burrows' office and came out with my complimentary pass. Good job I didn't have to go in and get it myself.

As a result of rehearsing; changing my behaviour by not drinking; and becoming champion in the 'Strictly Dodge Sylvester' contest, I arrived one Saturday night.

Picture the scene: the dance floor was packed with hundreds of my fellow teenagers waiting expectantly.

"Take your partners for the next dance, the foxtrot," Bert said, the band struck up and I launched into 'Love is a Many Splendoured Thing'.

This was it, I was living the dream! I'll never forget it! Up there, in the spotlight!

Hard to describe but it was unlike anything else I'd ever felt: I was a singer!

This failed student, bread delivery lad, electrician, and let's face it, not-so-hot plumber was finally doing something he was good at.

I sang regularly with the band and also tried my hand at the local club and pub scene as half of a double Act with Terry O'Connor, who told a good joke and played the piano accordion.

Every venue had a board outside that listed it's 'Forthcoming Attractions', a phrase that was open to dispute as far as our act was concerned

We were billed as 'The Two Terrys, Comedy and Song' because...

Terry played well and I could sing, but our comedy?.

Here's one example of our 'comedy':

Terry would start playing the Ballad of Davy Crockett (a big hit in the Fifties), I would appear from the gents' toilet at the back of the room and rush towards the stage wearing a Davy Crockett hat, (popular comedy headgear of the time, it looked like I had a dead badger wedged over my ears). To maximise the potential for hysteria, I also had an arrow sticking out of my chest.

Upon reaching the microphone, I would scream: "LOOK OUT, INDIANS".

Then, overriding the laughter which by now had reached fever pitch, I removed the arrow and calmly sang the rest of the song.

I'm blushing as I'm writing this!

CHAPTER 4
A SAINT AT LAST

I was on the bottom rung of the show business ladder and what's more (and this kept my folks happy), I also had a trade to fall back on. Plus, there was the rugby!

St Helens is a rugby league town and being a fit young lad, I became part of the local under-21 league, joining the Saints B Team and playing left wing.

An added bonus was that occasionally at Knowsley Road (the Saints' ground) we got to train with the first team alongside the legends: Alex Murphy, Vince Karalius and Duggie Greenall, to mention a few.

I did well at that level. I was quick, scoring regularly and although not fast (or tough) enough to go further, I am grateful that I got to wear the coveted 'Saints' red and white strip.

I was a busy boy now. There was the rugby, singing at the Co-op, the pub gigs with Terry and, oh yes, let's not forget the day job.

To become an indentured (resisting the teeth jokes) tradesman took five years, by which time the apprenticeship would have been served and you would go out into the wide world as a fully-fledged plumber.

It was thought best for the trainee to have a final task and therefore I was given my own house to 'plumb'.

It was a three-bedroomed end of terrace, soon to be occupied by a grateful St Helens family who had reached the top of the council house waiting list.

It was my baby. I'd done virtually all of the plumbing and now, the plastering and decorating having been completed, the day had arrived for my work to be put to the test. Time to turn the water on!

I nervously moved around the house for a half an hour or more, checking for leaks and apart from a dribble from an upstairs tap which I quickly fixed, all was well with my world.

I'd done it. Within a few days I would be a proper plumber, a man who, for the rest of his life, would always have a 'trade to fall back on'.

My reverie was interrupted by a wheezing sound.

It came from an elderly carpenter who was sitting at the bottom of the stairs. It sounded like he was having a coughing fit.

"Are you alright, Tommy?"

"Allreet, ahm moor tha allreet son, but I'll tell thee summat."

He was wiping away tears (of laughter): "Dustha' know, son, I've been in t'buildin' trade all me life and it's fost time I've seen watter cummin aht of a thirteen amp socket"

His finger pointed at the wall and I saw, to my horror, three little streams of water dribbling from the socket. Immediately I dashed into the kitchen to turn off the stop tap under the sink, en route I did a spot of aquaplaning through a pool of water forming directly underneath the ceiling light fitting.

Racing back on my way upstairs I became aware of another unique feature of this particular house: a shower in the hall!

In the bathroom, I flung open the cupboard containing the large copper cylinder and all became clear. In the top of the cylinder, a three-inch diameter immersion heater was normally fitted and to accommodate this appliance, a three-inch hole was drilled at the factory.

The problem was obvious: the hole was visible but the immersion heater was absent.

The system had filled to capacity but this young budding plumber had forgotten to fit the heater before turning the water on. The result was catastrophic.

For almost an hour, water had merrily flowed down from the hole into the floor space also finding it's way into the conduit pipes containing the electrics and by now the ceilings of the downstairs rooms were ready to collapse under the weight of water.

It was a total disaster! The house was waterlogged! I had created my own version of Atlantis.

The queues were already forming.

"Roll up, roll up, and welcome to Aqualand!"

"See how many varieties of marine life you can spot during your visit."

"Check out the waterfall in the airing cupboard."

"Marvel at the double rainbow in the kitchen."

Meanwhile the incoming tenants were down at the local diving club being kitted up with the best wetsuits and snorkels the council could afford.

More shame for me then. I was a laughing stock.

This episode probably sums up the whole of my school

and working life. I hadn't revealed any ability to learn back at West Park and was now turning out to be hopeless in the workplace.

The only talent I had was as a singer, along with a capacity for playing practical jokes and generally fooling around. But that could never become a trade… surely not!

CHAPTER 5
HER MAJESTY REQUESTS

ALTHOUGH more than twenty years would pass before we'd actually meet, the Queen did drop me a line in 1957 to ask if I fancied giving up on the plumbing and instead give her a hand defending the realm for two years. She called it National Service.

Naturally, I considered her request carefully and was finally persuaded to accept, following a series of letters from the St Helens Corporation Building Department, the Merseyside Ratepayers Association and the local Inshore Lifeboat crew. They all said my absence on the building sites would be noticed but that my country needed me and I should go... soon!

With all three branches of the Armed Forces clamouring for my services, I had a difficult decision to make.

The Royal Navy were disappointed to be turned down, but I felt that my recent water based experiences were enough to last me a lifetime.

As for the Army, I'd done a lot of underground pipe

and drain laying during the last five years and was prone to the odd twinge of 'Trench Foot'.

So the Royal Air Force it was to be. Yes, the skies above this Septic Isle would once again be safe, our enemies already quaking in their boots. And why: because the serried ranks of our brave boys in blue are about to be swelled by... a plumber.

I'd previously attended a medical exam and, in particular, an aptitude test that I must have passed with flying colours. (Aptitude...ya boo to you Mr Jacques).

RAF Cardington was the station that received the National Service intake. There we were, that May morning, lumped together from all walks of life; nervous, apprehensive and definitely homesick.

We were given uniforms, had regulation haircuts, got drunk most nights (I was introduced to 'Black Velvet', a mixture of Babycham and Guinness) and generally had a good time until, at the end of the week, we were loaded onto trains and unloaded at Wilmslow Railway Station in the heart of Cheshire. Which is where it all changed, for the worse.

We were greeted by several uniformed maniacs rushing up and down the platform roaring and screaming at us, sticking their red enraged faces into ours and bellowing orders which we couldn't understand and were too scared to question.

Wearing full uniform, including winter greatcoats and carrying full kitbags, we were frogmarched up a steep hill until we reached RAF Wilmslow.

Exhausted, bathed in sweat and trembling in fear, we stood in straggly lines awaiting our fate.

As one of the tormentors approached, I risked a quick sideways glance at him. In a flash he was in my face, eyes popping, crimson complexion now approaching purple.

Well, hello Corporal! This was 'Jock' Weir, my first sighting of a deranged Scottish person. Now in my time I'd survived the school thrashings, roughed it on the building site, even played rugby but right now I was dead scared.

This man really frightened me. Stockily built and not very tall, he was screaming up my nose.

I could see right down his throat, feel his spittle on my cheek, very nasty.

"YOU, YOU! WHO DO YOU THINK YOU'RE LOOKING AT ?"

Assuming the question was rhetorical, I declined to answer.

"YOU LOOK AT ME LIKE THAT AGAIN, LOFTY, AND YOUR FEET WON'T TOUCH."

That's the way it worked, once they'd reduced us all into a state of fear and trembling they could make us do anything. And so it carried on. We were constantly being screamed at in an effort to turn us into some form of cohesive unit. (I nearly said fighting force, but I couldn't keep me face straight!).

THE FIRST PAY PARADE

Our first test of cohesiveness loomed a few days after we arrived. We were going to be paid! In recognition that we were now an integral part of the Armed Forces, we were going to be paid our due… almost three quid a week!

The event was to take place the following day in a large hangar and we were taken in and rehearsed, to ensure we would be a credit to the uniform.

Lined up and stood at ease in three rows, we were told

that when we heard our name and last three numbers called we would a) snap to attention, b) march quickly to the paymaster's table, c) halt, d) slam the right foot down whilst standing rigid, e) fling up a salute and then f) bellow our name and number. We would then be handed our ransom and complete the ritual in reverse (but not march backwards cos that would be silly).

I've just counted back and that's at least half a dozen things to remember in quick succession. Quinn I might have been but quick to remember I weren't.

But I wasn't too concerned, the parade would be called alphabetically, surely, and by the time they got to Q I'd have seen the ritual a hundred times.

Approximately 500 strong, we were marched in and lined up as per rehearsal. In front of us was a long trestle table groaning under a mountain of coins of every denomination all arranged immaculately and piled in neat columns. Seated behind the table were several uniformed staff ranging from the humble pay clerks to various officers.

Corporal Purple was prowling up and down muttering (there's a novelty), informing us that any mistakes would be punishable by death or worse.

"PARAAADE" (deathly hush)

"PARAAADE" (even deathlier)

"ATTAAAAAAIIIIIIN.................SHUN" (we all did what the chap said)

"PARAAADE"

"STAND AAAT...............EASE " (at ease we stood – but at ease we weren't)

(Relax, Bernard, there's a hundred before you)

"648 QUINN AC2" (Whaaat the ****!)

"648 QUINN AC2" (BUT LOUDER)

Glaswegian spittle... incoming... starboard:

"YEW QUINN, ARE YEW DEEF OR SOMETHIN'?"

The table smiled, of course!. This was their happy hour.

"IN YOUR OWN SWEET TIME" (Corporal Peuce).

"ATTAAAIIIIN.....SHUN".

"LIPRYT, LYPRYT, LIPRYT, LIPRYT, LIPRYT, LIPRYT."

I approached the table at such a rate of knots, the smiles faded.

"HE'S TOO FAST! TOOO FAAAST!"

The floor was painted and highly polished. It was like a flaming skating rink. The boots were new, the studs were shiny: an accident waiting to happen!

All in a flash, I brought my feet together, flung up a salute: "648 Quinn AC2 SIR'"

KERRASH!!

The 'S' in 'SIR' left my mouth at exactly the same time I hit the table.

The table, which as I told you earlier, was stacked high with numerous bundles of pound notes and piled high with several hundred pounds worth of coins of the realm: half crowns, two bob pieces, shillings, tanners, threepenny bits and, oh yes, lots and lots of pennies.

All of these piles fastidiously arranged with military precision by the Pay Clerks to ensure a flawless and speedy Pay Parade.

On the Richter scale of one to ten, the table collision must have been worth a seven at least; several skyscrapers of coins swaying briefly then crashing in all directions. Then there was the 'after shock', coins rolling around on a highly polished surface, not to mention the sound of a strangled hysterical gurgle from four hundred throats.

I was barely able to move, managing to return to my place clutching my pittance: Two Pounds 'something', which had been begrudgingly handed over by one of the now chastened Paymasters.

Surprisingly, I was not punished for my part in the debacle. Obviously, I was blameless and on subsequent Pay Parades there was a noticeable lack of height in the arrangement of Coins.

It's also worth mentioning that during 'square bashing', most of us were having a bloody good time. I admit we didn't want to be there, were homesick, and two years seemed a long, long time but, along with many National Servicemen, I'm not alone when I say I had some of the best times of my life, but that's often the case looking back, isn't it?

One important aspect was that I was moving away from that 'worst plumber' tag… well, not quite!

One morning as rifle drill ended, our Corporal, 'Whispering Baritone' Weir, bellowed my name.

The second time that week. The first time he'd followed up by questioning my mental faculties,

"QUINN, YOU'RE THICK. WHAT ARE YOU?"

"I'm thick, Corporal".

I thought it best to agree because, at that very moment, of the sixty rifles in his view, mine was the only one that was being held aloft.

The other fifty nine had been grounded as part of a conspiracy to cause me acute embarrassment.

However, this time he merely roared, "REPORT TO SERGEANT WALLACE IN THE GENERAL STORES IMMEDIATELY."

Which I did, thinking I was to be issued with the RAF equivalent to a Dunce's Cap.

How wrong could I be?

Sergeant Wallace told me he'd been scanning our

records and discovered that I was a plumber and was from St Helens.

His suggestion was that, instead of spending every day on the parade ground, I would do some plumbing on a house he was renovating in Warrington (a few miles away) for a few hours each day for a week or so; and that this would also enable me to spend each night at home in St Helens (only a few more miles away).

He'd spoken with the Drill Instructors and they'd agreed to 'turn a blind eye'.

Naturally I leapt at the chance.

It sounded like a 'cushy number', and I'd heard about them from ex-servicemen on the site.

"Keep your eyes open for a 'cushy number'".

And one had just fell into my lap.

So for the next couple of weeks, I did some drill in the morning, 'plumbed' all afternoon in Warrington, and spent the evenings in the local pub with me mates.

Sadly, once my work had been completed, the plasterers and decorators moved in and I rejoined the Air Force for the last two weeks of basic training.

This involved a lot of hard work. I found the rifle choreography difficult to master but the fear factor helped.

We were also dropped off in the middle of the Peak District and left to survive for two days in a tent. That wasn't too bad, as we came across a remote pub and spent most of the time in an alcoholic haze.

Eventually, though, our last day at Wilmslow arrived, the passing-out parade was over and I set off home for a well earned week's leave.

As I approached the main gate I recognised Sergeant Wallace, he seemed somehow, well, different!.

"Hello Sarge".

"F*** off."

"Pardon."

"Don't f***in' hello sarge me, son".

"What's up?"

"I thought you said you were a f...in' plumber".

"Well, I am."

"Well, how come my house is under two foot of water"

"Two f***in' feet" (that was him again, not me).

"The decorators moved out last week, the carpet fitters finished yesterday, so last night I turned the water on." He was almost in tears.

"Fourteen f***in' leaks".

"Fourteen?" I tried to sound incredulous.

"Behind the bath, under the wash basin, the sink, everywhere you look there's a f***in' leak".

"Well it's never happened before," I lied.

"I'm really sorry," I said and I was.

But what could I do? I'd done the work to the best of my ability. I just wasn't any good!

I left the poor man shaking his head, almost in tears.

The euphoria of completing my basic training had disappeared and I was more determined than ever to become an ex-plumber.

It did cross my mind that he might send details of the events to my next posting and that retribution was waiting in some form or other, but happily that was the end of it.

WELCOME TO WILTSHIRE

The steam train clattered into Chippenham and we headed for a lorry that would deliver us to RAF Yatesbury. Fortunately, I'd met up with Brian Yates from the Wirral

Yes, I'm the one wearing his school blazer on holiday?

In Charles Street long before the bomb

Second row from the top, third rowm from the right.
Caned everyday – still trying to smile

Top row, second left – scruffy but still captain

Oh those teenage years, where did they go?

I'm second on the left (Sergent's bike on the right)

Another one bites the dust

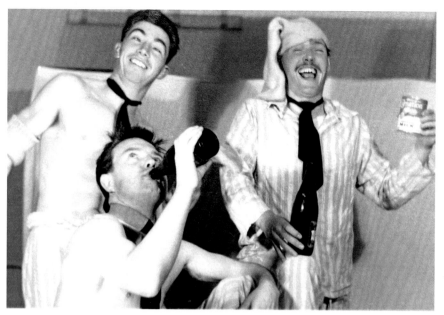

Pyjama party? We were bored

What a bunch of – smoothies!

Posing, moi?

We were broke, but we had it all

My very first

Charles Street.
Hitler started it – the council finished it

Charles Street rebuilt. Can you see the join?

who'd been with me at Wilmslow, so I didn't feel too lonely.

We were part of intake D10, twenty-odd blokes and we were billeted in Hut Y42. This would be home for the next six months of the next phase of our National Service, 'Trade Training'.

The following morning we assembled in a classroom. As you can imagine, with my academic history I was feeling slightly uneasy. While we were waiting for our instructor to appear, I asked the chaps around me what jobs they'd had in 'civvy street'.

Their answers depressed me somewhat, two or three BSc's in electronics and a couple of City and Guild electrical engineers.

I think it's time I told you what RAF Trade I was about to be trained in: I was going to be an Air Radar Mechanic. Brilliant: from plumbing to electronics!

This very dodgy plumber would be servicing aircraft bombing systems and not just any old bombers. No, they had saved me for the crème de la crème, the pointy end of the Nations defence: the V Bombers, the Vulcans, Victors and Valiants.

The ones that would drop H bombs on Russia, always on 24-hour alert, ready to fly if James Bond ever got it wrong.

Well, it was long before computers were used for assessment, so someone had looked at my entrance papers and decided I was wasted as a plumber.

The mental kink that had somehow got me through my 11-plus exam, resulting in four years of Grammar School misery, had surfaced again but this time the stakes were higher.

Anyone for World War Three?

The lectures started and I was lost. It was like going back to lower 3b and listening to algebra being explained. While all around me, classmates were making copious notes, I was staring out of the window wondering if Pat Boone would pip the Everly brothers to the No. 1 spot.

I had no idea what they were on about: airspeed, groundspeed, velocity, track, forward throw, etc. and no Arthur Cunningham to copy off. Corporal, you were right, I am thick!

The saving grace of my time in deepest Wiltshire was that we all had the same sense of humour and if any feeling of homesickness did surface it would quickly be submerged in a large measure of alcohol.

Once Friday night came, we were left to our own devices for 48 hours. Unlike Wilmslow, there was no spit and polishing or rifle drill; just plenty of spare time to study (joke); no one ever thought of working during the weekend.

So, on our first free Saturday, after a lie-in, wearing civilian clothes, we caught the bus to savour the delights of the best of the local fleshpots, namely the Chippenham NAAFI Club.

This was a venue built exclusively to provide entertainment for RAF personnel and it could hardly fail. In that small Wiltshire town on Saturday you couldn't move for RAF 'bods'.

They poured in from either Yatesbury, Melksham or Compton Bassett, all training centres for radar or radio technicians. There were thousands of us. You have to remember the Cold War was at its height and NATO needed strength in numbers to make the Russians nervous (good job they didn't have a spy in our midst).

So we set out to get pretty well smashed. The phrase

'binge drinking' hadn't been invented yet but whoever came up with it might well have used our session that evening as a reference point. The problem was that back home I drank beer, as you wouldn't be seen dead with a glass of cider in your fist, it was a big girl's drink. On the basis of 'When in Rome', however, we decided to sample the local cider, or 'scrumpy' as it's called.

We gave it not one ounce of respect. Big mistake, it was lethal! Apple-flavoured paint stripper!

"So moi deario, yer from up t'North and yew think yer 'ard dew yew".

Eight pints later we were carried on to the last bus. Half an hour passed, apparently, and then we disembarked (fell off) at the camp gates and crawled towards the security Guard Hut. We were queueing in the corridor leaning on each other, when word filtered back that there had been some thieving going on in town and we were all about to be searched.

I thrust my hands into the deep pockets of my Gabardine Mac and, to my horror, felt a number of 'trophies' I had filched from various taverns earlier. Nothing major: several beer mats, two or three ash trays, a couple of salt and pepper pots. I mean, for a man who, a few months earlier, had been re-enacting the Battle of Agincourt on a stolen bike in a dance hall, this was nothing.

But in my befuddled state, I knew I was in deep trouble.

I had to get rid of the booty. I was leaning on the wall opposite the office of the Head of the RAF Police, Flight Sergeant Dunlop. I'd never met him but he had a mean reputation and was not a man to cross swords with. His office door was open and quick as a flash I lurched in and emptied my pockets onto his desk. A moment later I was back leaning on the wall convulsed in giggles along with my comrades.

A few minutes later I was ushered into the 'search office' and confronted with a local policeman, an RAF officer and the Dunlop person. Upon seeing the officer, I banged my heels together and flung him an 'over the top' salute, nearly knocking myself over in the process.

"AIRMAN," shouted the Dunlop, "YOU DON'T SALUTE AN OFFICER WHEN YOU'RE NOT IN UNIFORM."

"Sorry, sarge."

"FLIGHT SERGEANT TO YOU, AIRMAN."

It wasn't going too well was it, but I was very drunk. I was duly searched and sent on my way.

We lay in our beds, drifting in and out of our respective stupors and howling with laughter when the 'trophies on the desk' incident was mentioned.

All was fine until the following morning when, apart from suffering the mother and father of all hangovers, we, the occupants of Hut Y42, were summoned en masse to the office of...you'll never guess who!

The previous night any mention of his surname provoked hilarious of comments, amongst them...

"Did you notice his INFLATED ego."

"He'll need to TREAD carefully."

"Can you imagine the size of his 'SKID MARKS'?"

But right now as we formed a silent, straggly line in that same corridor, nothing was funny any more. He hove into view, a man in his 40s, a Flight Sergeant in the RAF Police, absolutely immaculate, from the tip of his hat with the peak, flattened hard against his forehead, down past his white blanco'd belt and gaiters to his gleaming boots.

You could see your face in them and I was thinking I'd be seeing mine, up close, very soon.

He had a soft Scottish accent, nothing like the bellicose gravel of my previous tormentor, Corporal Weir, and yet somehow these dulcet tones were all the more menacing.

"So, what a sight we are this morning, aren't we?".

"A wee bit different from the jolly japers I met last night?"

"The jokers who thought they could walk into my office, MY OFFICE, and make a fool of me."

(I don't know about the others but I was scared).

"Well, let me tell you what's going to happen. Unless the culprit steps forward and admits his guilt NOW, all Leave at RAF Yatesbury will be cancelled this coming Friday."

(I thought for a second, 1500 blokes at least locked up for the weekend, nothing to do but hunt down the man responsible and then when they'd found him…well, let's not go there).

"YOU SEE, CHAPS, NOBODY MAKES A C**T OF CHIEFY DUNLOP."

I heard a little voice… it was mine!

"It was me, Flight Sergeant".

"STEP FORWARD THAT MAN."

and step forward he did.

"NAME AND NUMBER."

"5044648 A C 2 Quinn, Flight Sergeant".

"INTO MY OFFICE, AT THE DOUBLE".

Nice office I thought, immaculate, everything in it's place, tidy desk too, apart from some objects in the middle. He turned them over, with a ruler, as though touching them would somehow contaminate him with a deadly virus.

"SO YOU ADMIT THIS IS YOUR HANDIWORK"

"Yes, Flight Sergeant."

Well, I'd had my fun the night before and now it was his turn. He tore me off a strip or two, read me the riot act and an hour later I trudged out, humiliated, having to report the following morning to be officially charged with theft.

For the purpose of the proceedings, I had to be represented by an RAF officer, so there I was the following day sitting in this office with my QC by my side ready to appeal for clemency in case the black cap came out. Across the desk was the local constable and between us we completed my statement which detailed the previous evening's events.

"So you went into the Black Horse and you were in there for an hour or so, what did you have to drink during that time."

"Three pints of scrumpy."

Smiles all round.

"That's when you pocketed an ash tray?"

Then you went over to the Royal Oak for an hour.

"How much did you drink in there?".

"Another three pints of scrumpy, I think".

Chuckles from everyone except me.

"And that's when you took the salt and pepper pots?"

"And finally you found yourself in the Fox and Goose, what did you have in there?"

"Only another couple."

The laughter was hearty, and even I smiled.

"And that's when you took the rest of the ash trays".

"So, to sum up, you were in the village for two or three hours and in that time you drank up to eight pints of the local cider".

"That's right, Sir".

The place exploded! Surely, with all this hilarity, I was hoping I would get a free pardon.

Anyway, I pleaded guilty, signed the statement and waited for the inevitable summons…which never came! A few months later, at my next posting, I was called in to be told the charges had been dropped and warned 'as to my future behaviour'.

The irony was that on that fateful evening, they weren't looking for my pitiful souvenirs but for a quantity of silver plate that had been nicked from a large hotel nearby. What's more, the thief saw the police as he got off the bus and dropped the silverware in a ditch from where it was discovered later and handed back to its rightful owners.

So the whole episode ended thankfully without repercussions – but it did put me off cider for life.

However, life at Yatesbury was still interesting during the week. I lagged behind the rest of the class in the learning stakes but I was getting by and at least no one was caning me.

The difficulty came at the weekend. Our visits to Chippenham were rather subdued, for obvious reasons, and we found the rest of the time hard to fill. We overcame this by virtually wrecking the billet. It became a ritual. We would dismantle all the metal bed frames using a set of bike spanners and re-arrange them into a huge pyramid in the centre of the floor. Next we would drape ourselves in the sheets and pose on top of the edifice for photographs, a prize being awarded for the most bizarre image.

We were obviously 'stir crazy' but it helped to pass the time.

When the exams came round, our 'posse', about ten of us, failed miserably. We were hauled in front of a Wing

Commander and told we were a "threat to the discipline of the whole camp". (We dined out on that phrase).

He told us we had a choice of either being downgraded to the rank of catering assistants, which meant we would spend the next two years washing pots in the cookhouse, or we could retake the exam after a week's 'cramming'.

We all took the second option. At the end of that week, my brain was sore but it worked and I got through, soon to be upgraded to the dizzy height of AC1, (a first-class Airman was I).

We sat around waiting for our postings, the Scottish lads hoping for a ticket to RAF Lossiemouth. As for me, I was pretty certain there wasn't a V Bomber base within shouting distance of St Helens, most of them were in the flat bits of eastern England (nearer to Russia).

When I read that my posting was 'RAF Lindholme, Bomber Command Bombing School', near Doncaster, Yorkshire, I had to look at a map to find out where Yorkshire was, never mind Doncaster. (I jest, but at the age of 21, apart from two trips to Wembley, I'd never been out of my home county).

I had been on a school trip to the Lake District but after four hours of non-stop rain, Sister Gertrude thought it was a message from above and we turned back when we got to Morecambe.

I travelled to Yorkshire with Brian Yates, who had been posted to RAF Finningley, which is now called Robin Hood Airport, which is strange 'cos it's nowhere near Nottingham (but then again Russell Crowe did Robin Hood with an Irish accent), so what do I know? My posting, RAF Lindholme, is now a prison!

The highlight of the trip north was seeing Frankie Vaughan at Euston Station. He was wearing a camel hair coat and looked like the real star he was. Who'd have guessed that, 30 years later, me and Frank would become good friends and cruise together on the QE2?

I parted company with AC1 Yates on Doncaster Station and we were both pretty choked. We'd been together since day one at Cardington. Brian was the proud owner of a Vincent motor bike, astride which I'd ridden many a mile, if only as rear gunner. We promised to keep in touch and we did. The next time we met we were 25 years older. I was in panto near his home in Poole. He was an airline pilot, would you believe. (I told you they were all clever except me).

But that December night on 'Donny' station we were just two sad, lonely blokes.

THE RUSSIANS ARE COMING

I spent the first night at Lindholme in a transit billet. I knew no one and after the camaraderie I'd enjoyed at Yatesbury, I was like a fish out of water.

The following morning I was given a pack of tickets and had to do the rounds of the different departments to be signed in. Very boring – until I reached the accounts section. I was confronted by six foot five inches of Scottish enthusiasm called Pilot Officer James Morrison.

"Ah, come in Quinn, sit ye down the noo",

(Think I like him).

"I've been expecting you."

(Here we go I thought, it's the 'stolen ashtrays' here to haunt me already – but no!)

"I'm the rugby officer, it says on your records you played rugby league for St Helens".

"Only the B Team, sir," (which he ignored).

"What position?"

"Left wing, Sir."

"Excellent, and less of the sir".

"You'll have your boots, of course?"

"We're training tonight at 7, you're playing at Hemswell on Wednesday".

"See you in the Gym, 7 sharp, 10 press ups for every minute you're late".

And I was out the door.

That couple of minutes in the Office of 'Big Jim' set the pattern for the next year-and-a-half of my life. The RAF took their sport seriously and in my case it took priority over everything else.

I may have spent six months learning how to bomb Russia, but that was unimportant compared to how many tries I might score for the honour of the station.

Suddenly life was good again, my studying days were behind me, no more wrestling with maths and physics, I'd moved on and joined the team, not just any old team but the Station Rugby team. It might not sound much now but it changed my life.

The business of defending the realm was now in the hands of others.

All I had to do was defend my corner of the rugby pitch on Wednesday afternoon and every now and again pop up the other end and score the odd try, which I'm happy to say I did… frequently!

Our team did well, not least because 'big Jim', as we called our leader, the tallest stand-off I'd ever seen, had a hell of a kicking game, which as a League player I wasn't too pleased about.

I don't want to get too technical but, in those days,

there was a vast difference between the two rugby codes, League and Union.

In Union, which I was now playing, you were encouraged to kick the ball out of hand.

In League, where I had come from, kicking was rare. It was essentially a handling game.

The downside for me was that I spent a lot of time jogging up the touchline without the ball.

The good bit was we were often nearer the other side's try line so, when it came to scoring, I didn't have to run as far.

As for other differences between the two codes, the moment I knew for certain I was in another world came when, during play, I saw an opposing player (officer), take out a hankie from his shorts, blow his nose, replace the hankie and carry on playing. Never forgotten it!

Apart from the game itself, the social life was something else. A staggering amount of alcohol was consumed on the way home. Anyone who could disembark from the coach unassisted at the end of the evening was a traitor and in danger of being dropped from the squad. And not just after the game…

We were once flown down to RAF Marham in Norfolk for a seven-a-side tournament. It's a form of the game that requires intense dedication and superb fitness.

The night before I met up with Dave Smith, a mate from Yatesbury who had been posted to Marham. He took us to the local pub and we got absolutely legless.

The following day we could hardly walk, let alone play, needless to say we were eliminated early in the competition…and nobody seemed to mind!

I can't recall any kind of recrimination, it was part and

parcel of the culture at the time: you played, you drank, you drank, you played.

The Marham trip was unforgettable for another reason. Hungover and defeated, our team piled into a Varsity aircraft for the flight back to Lindholme. The twin-engined Varsity, known to all and sundry as the 'Pig', was used to train bomb aimers. It was early evening in May and we'd climbed to about 5,000 feet when the co-pilot came back and asked if anyone fancied doing a spot of bomb aiming. Thinking it was a chance of sitting up front with the pilot, I put my hand up. I stood up to move forward when he did no more than lift up a huge panel in the floor.

"Down you go, Biggles."

I peered nervously through the hole and there, as flat as ever, was Norfolk in all its glory, viewed through a perspex pod attached to the belly of the aircraft by means of a few hundred rivets.

To the jeers of my team mates, I gingerly lowered myself to lie face down on the perspex but I couldn't help noticing that the rivets weren't all that big and that the perspex was showing signs of wear and tear. On a buttock-clenching scale of one to ten, I gave this a twelve.

There I was lying on me stomach looking straight down, nothing between me and our green and pleasant land except a mile and half of fresh air and a bit of plastic. What a way to cure a hangover!

Notwithstanding our seven-a-side performance, the weekly routine remained the same and the time flew by.

I was able to get home most weekends by using the coach that left the front gate on Friday afternoon bound for Manchester Piccadilly. From there I'd finish the trip by 'hitching' which, in those days, wasn't difficult. There were thousands of young men doing National Service and while wearing 'civvies' you'd have your RAF beret in your pocket and plonk it on your head when needed. This usually did the trick, most drivers then were sympathetic to servicemen, especially the truckers who were grateful for a bit of company.

I remember one bloke showing me how he rested his right leg on long journeys. When he reached 'cruise' speed he produced a piece of timber, cut to size, and wedged it between the accelerator and the door handle, leaving both feet free. Health and safety – what's that?

Following a weekend at home with me mates, I had to be in Piccadilly by midnight Sunday for the return coach trip, which is when fate dealt me a kind hand.

The chap who organised the coach came from St Helens and as he was due to be demobbed, asked me if I fancied taking it over: "there'll be a few bob in it for you."

He showed me the routine.

During the week I would take bookings, ring up the coach depot and tell them roughly how many seats were needed.

As the coach set off on Friday afternoon, I would go round like the bus conductor I was born to be and collected the cash: fourteen shillings return. On the return from Piccadilly, it was ten shillings for a single, (usually those who had skived off early on Friday).

Quite often the coach would be overloaded on the way back, literally standing room only, but sit or stand, it was still 'ten bob'. We would get back to camp as dawn was breaking, maybe three hours later, an horrendous trip if you were standing but nobody complained, it's just the way it was.

But this is where it got interesting. My brief was to give the driver 20 quid for his boss, a quid for himself and I could keep the rest. If that sounds ridiculously cheap, remember that in the Fifties, if you earned twenty pounds a week you were doing very nicely. My take-home pay from the RAF was almost three pounds!

So in the early hours of that first Monday morning I sat on the back seat and tipped out the 'take'. I counted out twenty-one pounds and gazed in disbelief at the mound of coins that was mine. I hastily shovelled it into my holdall, not daring to count it.

The driver seemed happy as he took his share: "see you next week."

With heart racing, I legged it to the billet. Once inside, sitting on the toilet for privacy, I counted out my winnings. Unbelievable: twelve pounds ten shillings!

For doing practically nothing I had earned a month's pay in one weekend.

Marvelling at my good fortune, I promptly opened a Post Office Savings Account.

The good news was repeated week after week and I was such a happy bunny. As the rugby season ended, I became an essential part of the sprint relay team, meaning more time off from my day job. The summer of '58 was such a happy one for me.

Come October, though, and my life was to change forever.

We had played and beaten RAF Norton, a station on the edge of Sheffield. On the way back, we stopped for the usual Olympic Drinking event, following which some of us decided to disembark in Doncaster Town centre and visit the local dance, specifically at the Baths (a lot of towns boarded over their swimming pool in the winter and opened the venue as a dance hall).

I was pretty drunk and weaved my way over to the

first pretty girl I saw. She agreed to dance with me but wouldn't tell me her name or give me her number.

However Cupid, in the shape of her friend Maureen, gave me the necessary info. Her name was Madge and she worked in Accounts at the Nuttall's Mintoes Sweet Factory.

The following day I phoned her and talked her into a 'date' the following weekend, which by the way would mean giving up being a coach proprietor.

I was smitten, folks. 'Something gotta hold of my heart' as the song went.

My life changed. I gave up on the coach earnings, started staying in Doncaster at weekends and began thinking of becoming a singer rather than a plumber.

I mean, let's face it, I had every chance of becoming better at singing than plumbing.

As the Queen Mother used to say: "a complete no-brainer!"

FLIGHT SERGEANT'S BIKE AND BURMA QUEEN

It was a cold, dismal December morning. A gale swept across the deserted runways, leaving the windsock horizontal, the skies were grey and threatening to unload torrents of freezing rain.

Not a day, you might think, to embark on a cycling tour of South Yorkshire. It was a Sunday, the bus service from RAF Lindholme to Doncaster was non-existent, so I had to rely on native cunning, in other words I was going to 'borrow' the Flight Sergeant's bike. Yes this lowly National Serviceman, Quinn, Bernard, Senior Aircraftsman 5044648, was about to commit a court martial offence.

Flt Sergeant Long was a kindly soul who tolerated my

presence in his section with good humoured patience. He only saw me a couple of days a week, the rest of the time I was doing more important things, like playing rugby for the station team, (more important than defending the realm).

RAF Lindholme was the Bomber Command Bombing School, so what was a thick, dodgy plumber doing at the pointy end of Britain's Nuclear Deterrent, you might ask. I know, I asked the same question a hundred times, especially when I was struggling to make head or tail of Faraday's Law during my Radar exams.

Now the section that Flt Sgt Long ran was responsible for servicing the cameras that were on board every training flight. What happened was this: the School Aircraft would take off crammed full of H Bomb aiming gear and a few student navigation and bomb aiming officers. They would climb to about 12,000 feet and then pick a target. (At this point I should make it clear that these were dummy runs. Even though we were in the middle of the Cold War, no bombs were carried at any time.)

The target could be any major landmark in the country. One day it could be the Forth Bridge, the next day Bournemouth Pier. Come to think of it, even if they had been carrying bombs, it would have been a waste of the taxpayers' money to have actually destroyed one of our piers. I mean, a combination of Town Councils run by accountants; television's refusal to give real talent a chance; and successive governments giving millions to the 'arts' but neglecting to support 'family entertainment' have rendered piers redundant anyway. (Sorry, I went off on one then, didn't I?)

So there they were, heading for the target not in a Victor, which were expensive to run and we only had a few. No, what the School had was an old, four-engine propeller driven Hastings bomber done up inside like a Vulcan. This is where our Section came in, as every dummy run at every target was filmed by our cameras set above the radar screen in the aircraft. After each flight we would collect the camera, have the film developed and the students would be marked on the accuracy of their Bombing Run. I'm sorry to have gone on about all this bombing stuff but if you were paying taxes in 1958, you know where your money went now!

So let's get back to Flt Sgt Long and why I was about to steal/borrow his bike. The Bombing School operated on a five-day week, Monday to Friday (surely the Russians knew that so why didn't they attack us one weekend, it would have been a walkover!). "Aw, come on, Ivan, that's not fair, it's bloody Saturday! When are we expected to do the shopping and take the kids to the pictures, for God's sake? Come back on Monday and we'll make a game of it, alright."

Flt Sgt Long never used his bike at the weekend, it was left parked in the bike rack, so I wasn't depriving him of it, was I? And the fact was, I had my first singing job that Sunday. A local agent was giving me a 'try out'.

The venue was a Working Men's Club in a mining village a few miles out of Doncaster and without the pushbike, I'd never have made it.

So out into the chill I went, leaving behind the doubtful comforts of my billet, Tedder Block 4. I was wearing my light grey, double breasted Gabardine Mac, it was the fashion item to die for in those days, and underneath it my 'stage suit'. Well, I say 'stage suit' but I only had the one and tonight it was going to have to pass itself off as stage wear.

I also had stuffed down the front, a soft leather folder containing piano copies of my entire musical repertoire, about 12 sheets in all (3 spots, 4 songs a spot, more than adequate for a fledgling pub singer).

The songs ranged from my up-tempo opener, 'That old Black Magic', to my favourite tear jerker, 'The Twelfth of Never'. How could I possibly fail, I hear you cry!

I approached the bike rack and there it was, his trusty (waiting to be stolen) steed, before mounting, I stooped to put on my very own pair of 'bicycle clips' as remember, I was wearing my 'stage suit' and the bike didn't have a chain guard.

Eventually arriving at the venue, I was nonplussed to find my name Bernie Quinn wasn't listed on the 'Today's Entertainment' notice board. Instead, I read (in coloured chalk) 'Exotic Dancer BURMA QUEEN'. It slowly dawned on me what had happened: BERNIE QUINN had become BURMA QUEEN.

Blind panic overtook me as my predicament became clear. Even in my confused state, it was clear that some kind of 'glitch' had occurred in the booking, resulting in an inexperienced male crooner with just a handful of songs in his repertoire, about to face an audience of men, the worse for drink, expecting to see a woman take her clothes off.

Fantastically funny, except for one thing… that crooner was me.

There was no way out! I'd already been confronted by the club secretary who'd assumed I was the stripper's manager or similar. An easy mistake to make, I was the only person he'd seen that day wearing a Gabardine Mac and carrying a leather briefcase. I explained the situation to him before attempting to bid him adieu (but not in French),

"Weer dus tha' think thar guin? Tha'll av to go on and

do summat, if I doant give this lot sum kind of show they'll tear t'place apart."

I'd looked around and worked out that whilst even the total destruction of all the fixtures and fittings in the pub wouldn't cause the Insurance Company's shareholders any sleepless nights, nevertheless he did have a point. My worry was that, if I was within range (like up on the stage) there was every likelihood they'd start on me once they'd finished with the furniture.

"Doan't worry lad, ah'll soffen t'blow wen ah annahnce thi. Na' get thissen reddy wi' ar pianerist."

Ice cold sweat running down my back, I'd given my music to the 'pianerist' who thought the whole thing was highly amusing, but then he would be hidden from the audience by the piano, wouldn't he? I thought I'd have the secretary on my side to 'soffen t'blow', but that didn't happen. This was his introduction...

"NA' THEN LADS, IF THA'LL SHURRUP FOR A MINUTE, WE'LL GERRON WI'T'SHOW. THERE'S BIN A COCK UP WI' T'AGENT AN' T'STRIPPERS NOT CUMMIN." (Neanderthal roar of anger)

"SHURRUP AND LISTEN. IT WERE A SIMPLE SPELLING MISTAKE, COULD APPEN TO ANYBODY, YOU'RE NOT GETTING A STRIPPER CALLED BURMA QUEEN, YOU'RE GETTING A SINGER CALLED BERNIE QUINN." (A riot starts and murder will surely follow)

"GIVE THE POOR BUGGER A CHANCE....BERNIE QUINN."

FIRE BELL RINGS CONTINUOUSLY: SADLY NOT IN SAME KEY AS THE INTRO TO 'THAT OLD BLACK MAGIC', AND I WAS ON.

And, strangely enough, after the first few choruses of "Cumon Burma, Gerrem Off, Gerrem Off" and a lot of derisory whistles and catcalls, they allowed me to live. The ones that stayed, about half the audience, saw the funny side and tolerated my offerings.

I didn't get any applause and sang to a constant hubbub of noise and indifference, but I survived.

Perhaps they were used to regular 'cock ups', (though not on my scale) and had been conditioned to take them in their stride.

I never found out how it happened and naturally I complained, but no one seemed to know or really care: "these things happen, it's show business, get used to it or get out of it" was the nearest I got to sympathy in the agent's office.

The direct consequence of my trauma, though, that I worked out on my return journey, was that I did change my stage name from Quinn to 'Clifton'.

My Dad was not best pleased: "What's wrong with 'Quinn'? It's been good enough for generations of us."

That's true, Dad, but you weren't there in that club that Sunday in 1958.

And I can almost hear his voice, as I'm writing this: "Sunday lunchtime, did you say, did you miss Mass, Bernard?"

Yes, Dad, I did miss Mass… so perhaps I deserved it!

CHAPTER 6
CIVVY STREET BECKONS

Opinions are divided amongst the generations of young men compelled to do their two years' National Service. Taken from their jobs and relationships for that amount of time proved difficult for many. In my case it was different. Of course I missed my family and was very homesick for a while but I wasn't in a relationship and I certainly didn't have a career.

Whats more, I'd been given the chance to break free from an uncertain future as an awful plumber. Fate had dropped me right in the heart of northern clubland and I'd enjoyed my first taste of it.

The first thing I did after my demob was give all my plumbing tools to my younger brother Michael, who was becoming a 'proper' plumber and, armed with an armful of sheet music and a decent suit, I set off on a career in show business.

SOHO AUDITION

As the Sheffield train clanked slowly out of Doncaster Station, I had to agree with the ticket collector: "It wor a grand May morning."

To me, as a recently demobbed RAF National Serviceman, it looked like 1959 was going to be a great year. I was travelling back home to St Helens following a weekend singing in the South Yorkshire working men's clubs. I had earned, wait for it, around £15, as much as many men would get for a full five-and-a-half day working week. I was tall, dark and average, had a full mop of dark hair and was blessed with a good singing voice.

My stage act, which at that time had no comedy in it (there's a blessing), consisted of most of the current popular ballads by Johnny Mathis, Eddie Fisher, Dean Martin, Al Martino, etc, and had been well received by audiences of mainly miners and their wives.

I leaned back in my seat, newspaper in hand, dressed casually in sports coat and flannels and as the steam locomotive nudged noisily past the Hexthorpe Plant Works, I could actually see men working for a living.

Yet here I was, a 23-year-old ex-plumber, actually living the dream, I was a professional singer!

Let's face it, I was an awful plumber, probably the worst ever employed by St Helens Corporation. I left a trail of leaks behind me wherever I went. Conditions on building sites I worked on were being compared to the Battle of the Somme. I was a one-man Merseyside Tsunami. Matters came to a head when the entire team of plumbers employed to follow me to sort out the mess went down with trench foot!

I really wanted to stop being a Plumber, (a sentiment

that was shared, I'm sure, by the entire Council Building Department, not to mention the long-suffering St Helens ratepayers); plus I'd given my tools away, so no going back.

So as the train gathered speed, I looked again at 'The Stage' newspaper, particularly at the advert that would surely mean my plumbing days were over…

ALAN GALE PRODUCTIONS REQUIRE LIGHT BARITONE FOR LONG SOUTH COAST SUMMER SEASON. OPEN AUDITION, MAX RIVERS REHEARSAL ROOMS, GREAT NEWPORT ST. SOHO. WEDNESDAY 10AM. BRING OWN MUSIC.

(Turned out Alan Gale had a son who went on to T.V fame as a Blue Peter presenter, namely Peter Duncan.)

"This is it," I thought, "I'm a light baritone, I'm a good singer, I'm a better singer than I am a plumber." (Perhaps not the best reference).

So, to London! But how?

I'd been before, twice. Admittedly on the two previous occasions I'd graced the capital with my presence, I'd been garbed from head to foot in red and white, was twirling a large rattle and roaring "COME ON YOU SAINTS!", but facts were facts.

Now had you been with me on that train you might have pointed out that Wembley Stadium was a long way from Soho and that the Rugby League Cup Final was, in many ways, certainly culturally and artistically, a fair distance from a twice-nightly revue on Bournemouth Pier. But I wouldn't have listened because I was on the verge of being a full-time professional performer in…The Business we call Show!!

It was Monday; the audition was Wednesday morning, so I would hitch hike.

Back in the Fifties 'thumbing' was an accepted method of travel. So the following afternoon, wearing the same sports coat and flannels but carrying a suitcase containing my 'stage' suit, I hopped off the bus on the outskirts of St Helens and strode confidently past a large sign which read... Sutton and Sons, Long-Distance Hauliers.

My reasoning was thus...

a) I needed to get to London as quickly and as cheaply as possible.

b) Suttons had lots of lorries which travelled long distances, including London.

c) Simple: just walk in there and get a lift!

The outer office was full of men in overalls, mechanics and drivers I guessed, preparing for their overnight trips. I was getting a few funny looks, perhaps it was the rakish way I had left my collar up on my open-necked shirt (well, it looked good on Elvis!).

Soon it was my turn at the counter, manned by a large, sweaty harrassed man, probably the manager. He was smoking, as was everyone else in the room except me.

"WELL??"

His harsh bronchial rasp cut through the smoke filled haze like a chainsaw through a cabbage. The room fell silent.

"Erm, I'd like a lift to London please".

"YOU'D LIKE A WHAT?"

The silence, which had just fallen, descended even further, to a depth of silence that hadn't been plumbed since Oliver Twist asked for seconds or since Emperor Nero rose to his feet in the Coliseum and raised his thumb to indicate the fate of the wretched Christian before him.

"Erm...a lift to London...please?"

I felt my colour rising, passing my confidence which was heading in the other direction at a fair rate of knots.

"DID YOU HEAR THAT LADS? THIS JOKER WANTS A LIFT TO LONDON!"

A hoot of derision, from a score of smokers' throats, reverberated around the room.

"HERE LADS, UNLESS A'M MISTAKEN, THAT SIGN OUTSIDE T'DOOR SEZ, SUTTON AND SONS, LONG DISTANCE HAULIERS, DUNNIT?"

"YEAYYYYY!"

The colour rose to my cheeks as my spirits sank to my boots.

"WELL, THIS CHARACTER CAN'T F*****' READ, 'COS HE THINKS IT SEZ...SUTTON AND SONS, LONG DISTANCE F****' FREE TAXI SERVICE!!"

"NOW F*** OFF OUT OF MY OFFICE, SONNY JIM, WHILE YOUR STILL IN ONE F*****' PIECE."

My humiliation complete, I crept out of the door; if it had been locked I'd have slid under it.

My head ringing, I made for the bus stop.

"Hang on a minute, son", came the call from behind.

One of the drivers had followed me out and he seemed friendly. "You've got balls, lad, I'll say that, but if you wanna get down to London, you're goin' about it wrong way".

"Here's what to do, walk down t'road about half a mile till you come to that bridge over t'canal and wait at t'side of t'road. Lorries'll start comin' out in about an hour, stick your thumb out, you might get lucky...hey, and after what that bastard's just put you through, I hope you do".

I stammered some thanks, set off and reached the bridge.

After half an hour or so I regained my composure and

my spirits began to rise. Boy, that was tough, but perhaps that was part of the struggle you had to go through to get to the top in Show Business.

My reverie was broken by the sound of a lorry approaching. More in hope than anticipation, I hung out my thumb.

With a squeal of brakes, it stopped twenty yards past me. I ran forward, reached up and opened the nearside door. Before I had a chance to open my mouth, the driver, large, round-faced, jovial and smoking, of course, said: "Call me clairvoyant, but you wouldn't be wantin' a lift to London would you?.

"Please!"

"Hop in."

I did.

Norman, the driver, had also been witness to my ordeal and was even more sympathetic when he learned of my reasons for heading south.

In those days before the motorways were built, the journey took twelve hours and I hardly slept a wink as it was so uncomfortable.

The engine was in the cab and the noise was unbearable but I could hardly complain, could I?

Eventually around 6.30am we arrived at the Finchley Lorry Depot in North London. I joined Norman for a wash and brush up, and then while he headed for a hostel to sleep, I set off for the West End via the tube. Before we parted company, he advised me to be at the Finchley depot no later than 6pm if I needed a trip back home.

Looking back, I must have been exhausted but I don't remember feeling that tired. I guess I was running on pure adrenalin.

Following some confusion finding the right train,

9.30am found me having eggs and bacon in a cafe in Great Newport St. I'd already changed into my stage suit in a public toilet and although nervous for the audition, after all I'd been through in the last 24 hours there was no going back.

Not wanting to be first up, at about 10.15am I joined the queue of hopefuls on the stairs leading to the 2nd floor.

The Max Rivers Rehearsal Rooms was a warren of studios, some small, some large, with no evidence of sound proofing, even from the queue I could hear noises emanating from different sources, an overstrung piano from one, tap dancing from another, musical scales being sung elsewhere and so on.

I was like a fish out of water, after all I was just a 'turn' and here I was listening to all these frightful 'lardies' spouting on.

"I don't really need the work dahling, mmmm, I was going to stay in town for the summer and go up for a couple of BIG shows, but then I saw this and, of course, Alan knows my work and even though he doesn't need to hear me sing I thought I'd pop along anyway. It's Bournemouth isn't it? I hope so, I've got a friend who has a flat there, so cheap digs for me then."

Thank God they didn't speak to me. I wouldn't have known what to say. I mean they were from another planet, all this stuff about 'staying in town and not needing the work'. Why not own up? It was the middle of May and any artiste worth their salt would have been booked solid for the summer in those days unless, of course, you were me, who, having conquered the Doncaster Working Men's Club circuit was now about to have them falling at my feet on the south coast. Re 'cheap digs', it wouldn't matter to me if it was Bournemouth, Brighton or even bloody

Bognor because I didn't know anybody who lived south of Widnes.

Ooer! I'm next!

I walked in the studio briskly, outwardly exuding confidence I hoped. The room was basic even to a working class lad from the north: bare boards, the walls hadn't had a lick of paint since before the war, (I mean that one with Zeppelins) and was musty with the smell of stale cigarette smoke. Neither was Max Rivers familiar with the accepted northern concept called...window cleaning!

"Got your music?" asked one of the men standing by the window.

I produced a couple of copies.

"You'll only need the one."

"Erm, 'Scarlet Ribbons', I think."

"Give it to Charlie, then." (Charlie? Where is he?).

From behind the ancient upright piano in the corner of the room appeared an even more ancient and not so upright wizened hand, which snapped its fingers. Assuming it to be the hand of the invisible (and perhaps, not long for this earth) Charlie, I gave it my copy of the popular ballad of the time, 'Scarlet Ribbons', with a photograph of Harry Belafonte on the front cover. There was a grunt from behind the piano, like a voice from beyond the grave?

"This is it," I thought, "It's all I'm gonna get, you'd better go for it, Bernard, and I did."

"I peeked in to say goodnight," (I'm singing now, folks),

"and then I heard my child in prayer,"

'"and for me some scarlet ribbons for my hair',"

"If I live to be a hundred..."

"THANK YOU VERY MUCH, LEAVE US YOUR DETAILS, WE'LL LET YOU KNOW."

"Pardon!"

"JUST WRITE YOUR ADDRESS AND PHONE NUMBER IN THE BOOK, WE'LL LET YOU KNOW."

As if to confirm my sad demise, the Grim Reaper's claw appeared over the piano waving Harry Belafonte's photo at me in some form of sadistic farewell. I was absolutely devastated, having just got over the Sutton and Sons debacle of the previous day, here we go again.

"Was it not what you're lookin' for, then?"

"Oh you were fine, just leave us your details and er…

"You'll let me know, right?"

"Of course, of course…"

I made my exit down the stairs with a degree of dignity, I think, passing the queue of 'hopers', 'no hopers', 'past its' and 'neverwassers' (all of whom had been privy to every moment of my crucifixion) with my head held high.

And that was almost that!

Back up to Finchley, made rendevous with our Norman and twelve hours later, trudged up our garden path to collide with my brother John, who was on his way to work,

"How did it go, Bern?"

"They're gonna let me know "

And would you believe it…they never did!

VACUUM CLEANER SALES

So, having worked out that my immediate future wouldn't involve a season in Bournemouth, I weighed up my options and decided that I would spend it in another, perhaps less popular, resort that I know, Doncaster!

Whilst I admit it lacked some of the attractions of the

south coast town like theatres, a pier and a beach, nevertheless Doncaster had erm...I'll tell you what it had, WORK!

Yes, there was a pub or a club on almost every street corner and this gave a budding superstar like me an opportunity to perform whilst being, how shall I put it, not very good: well, okay at times, but pretty damn bad on occasions!

So the following Friday morning I was ready to set off, leaving behind the comfort of my family home. Looking back, I often wonder what my parents made of what I was up to. In fact I don't need to wonder because me Mam told me.

"Bernard, whatever has come over you I don't know, I really don't. You're giving up a perfectly good job. You're actually giving up your trade. There'll always be plenty of work for plumbers Bernard (you were dead right with that one Mam).

"Bernard", she sighed (and how well I remember these words), "you're going to the Devil".

To be fair to me Mam, you have to remember that nobody in our family circle had ever done what I was about to do. You got a trade (if you were lucky), and then you stayed in work until you were 65. And you were grateful!

Unhappy though I was to see her upset, I knew I had no choice. Having already been a contender for the title... 'Worst Pupil, West Park Grammar School', I really didn't want to go to my grave with another doubtful honour. (Replace the words 'Pupil and West Park Grammar School' with 'Plumber and St Helens Corporation').

I knew I had a talent and could sing well but more than

that, I knew that if I didn't get away and give it a chance, I would regret it for the rest of my life.

As for Mam's feelings, I'm glad that she lived to see me become successful in my chosen career not to mention being happily married with four great kids.

Anyway, with this supportive send-off ringing in my ears, off I headed, undaunted, in sports coat and flannels, Gabardine Mac (yes, that one) over my arm and stage suit in a case.

I used the following method: I caught a bus to the East Lancs Road and hitched a lift towards Manchester, then another bus, (or buses), till I got to the eastern side of the city, then hitching again in the direction of Sheffield. The usual mode of transport would be by lorry and I remember that sunny Friday afternoon sitting high and not so mighty in a lorry cab that reeked of diesel. As we climbed slowly up the Pennines, I saw travelling in the opposite direction a familiar looking Morris Minor soft top coupe and in it were five young men who only a couple of weeks earlier had been sharing a barrack room with me at RAF Lindholme. It made me realise how my life was changing.

Dropping off on the western edge of Sheffield, it was time to cross the city via a couple of trams before the final 'hitch' to my digs in Doncaster: No. 15 Royal Avenue was in the middle of a row of terraced houses a few minutes' walk from the town centre. It was owned by Mrs Best, and I was renting her back bedroom.

So here I was, bridges burned, no more plumbing surely. I was a singer…who was about to starve!

Welcome to the real world, Bernard. I had rent to pay, food to buy and had to clothe myself in a manner suitable to a rising star. There was only one thing for it…A DAY JOB!

I scanned the Situations Vacant columns in the Doncaster Free Press and there it was, leaping off the page at me: "SALES REPS WANTED BY WELL KNOWN LOCAL RETAIL CHAIN TO START IMMEDIATELY".

I devoured the details: generous basic wage plus attractive commission paid to successful applicants who must be smart, presentable and ambitious. Company car included, flexible hours.

Perfect! All boxes ticked, I said to myself, as I entered the premises of Mathews and Wrights, Electrical Appliance Retailers, Hallgate, Doncaster.

I was presentable and smart, very smart. After all, I was wearing my one and only mohair (singer's) suit, one that would be more at home topping the pop charts rather than the sales charts.

The firm's blue vans with gold lettering lined the street outside but I was more interested in the type of car I would be offered. (Driving licence? Don't bother me with details).

The co-owner Derek Wright was also wearing a Mohair suit although I doubted that he too was an aspiring pop star. Perhaps it was our shared sartorial taste that eschewed the formal interview because he looked me up and down and said: "When can you start?"

"Anytime"

"Right, our Mr. Edwards will fill you in… KEN."

The man in question (another snappy dresser) hove into view and led me towards one of the vans, opened the back door and said,

"Jump in; Bernard will mark your card".

So in I jumped and, squatting on the wheel arch (no seats), tried to unscramble my brain.

What about the basic salary, the generous commission rates, the company car?

Sitting across from me on the offside wheel arch was a fellow 'Sales Rep', (read on to discover the unfolding irony of that title) also a Bernard, (no conflict here, remember I was now a Bernie).

He introduced himself and I duly had my 'card marked'. For a start there had never been a basic salary. It was purely a ploy to get people to apply for the job. No one in the history of the firm had ever had one; it was, as he succinctly put it..."Sell or Starve Mate, Sell or Starve!" It also dawned on me that I was not on my way to becoming a 'Sales Representative', but more of a 'Door-to-Door Vacuum Cleaner Salesman'. (Oh dear, I could hear me mother's prophesy coming true: "You're going to the Devil, Bernard."

At that moment I thought she might have a point. After all, plumbing was a steady job, it was a trade, something to fall back on.

From her generations' standpoint there was nothing like a trade, it was a 'proper job' for life! But her number three son had turned his back on security and was all set to become a Chancer, a Neer-do-well, a Vacuum Cleaner Salesman, for God's sake, bringing down shame on the family name, so it's at least three Hail Mary's at Holy Cross on Sunday to bring me back from the clutches of Satan himself!

Meanwhile, back on the wheel arch, I listened as my first day 'on the knocker' was taking shape.

I was to 'shadow' Bernard.

"Stick wi' me, kid, oi'll put yow roit'," (no, not Norwegian, he was a Brummie),

'"Oh, and keep yer mouth shut, not a word, alroit."

The Bylock President 500 Watt Vacuum Cleaner, I was to discover, was the star 'seller'. For a start, every time you sold one you got a fiver, so one sale a day would bring you £25 a week at a time when a tradesman, (ie plumber, are you listening Mam?), would be earning £20 a week.

The '500' retailed at £35 and Bernard had a brand new one under his arm as he knocked on the first door of the 'Prop' (property), he'd been allocated. The semi-detached was on a large estate north of Doncaster which had been built, like hundreds of others throughout the country during the post-war years, in the so-called 'baby boom' period.

FLATTERY GETS...YOUR FOOT IN THE DOOR.

The door was opened by a young 30-ish attractive woman,

"Alroit Luv, is yer Mum in?"

"Wot dyer mean is me Mum in, this is my house."

"Get away, it corn't be, yer not owld enough."

"Cheeky!"

HE WAS AWAY...so on he went. Black Country's very own Charlie Charm convincing her that he wouldn't, nay, couldn't sell her this Vacuum Cleaner because it was for demonstrations only and if she allowed him through the door to demonstrate it and signed his 'Demo' Form he would be able to feed his kids this week.

HE WAS IN...and once inside the cheek continued.

"Is that sumbody whistlin' in the kitchen, luv?"

"I can't hear anythin'"

"Oh, it might be yer kettle then, did yer leave it on?"

"You cheeky devil, do you want a cup o' tea then?"

"Twist me arm, then, no sugar tho', a'm sweet enough."

As I watched the maestro perform, sitting back on the sofa drinking tea and making small talk, it occurred to me that the '500' had not emerged from its box. I felt I should mention the product but I'd been ordered to keep quiet.

Eventually curiosity got the upper hand and she asked about it.

GENIUS AT WORK...he broke open the box to reveal the cylinder still in its plastic, didn't unwrap it fully but instead found out when the husband would return from work (the 'pit'), arranging to call back then and 'demonstrate' to them both.

As we left the house minus the cleaner he told me his strategy. Get indoors by any means fair or foul, leave the '500' behind and only return when they're both in.

The process was repeated a couple more times in the neighbouring houses and at the appointed hour we returned.

The husband spoke first from behind a large mug of tea,

"You're wasting your time, mate, I've told her we're not havin' one, we can't afford it."

Not an encouraging start, in fact water off a duck's back to Bernard, who unwrapped the '500' as if the man hadn't spoken, found the nearest socket and started the demo.

Brilliant: the 500 watt motor roared into life and in one movement he removed the cap to reveal the bag, lifted the cylinder above his head and by means of the suction, attached the whole thing to the ceiling and walked away, leaving it there.

His audience, a married couple, plus one trainee salesman, watched open mouthed as the performance took place. It really was jaw-dropping stuff as, shouting above the noise of the motor, he explained it was the most powerful cleaner on the market,

"By the way, yow can't boy these in the shops," he shouted as he circled the scene.

It was like watching some kind of demented Music Hall plate spinner.

We watched, transfixed, waiting for the thing to detach itself bringing half the ceiling down but it held on until he switched it off and placed it on the floor.

Within a few seconds and without a word, he had fitted the attachments and gone to work on the carpet. No more than a minute later he switched it off and emptied the contents of the bag onto the carpet. I must say it was impressive: a huge mound of dirt was revealed!

CHAPTER 7
LET BATTLE COMMENCE

Those doorstep battles, and there were many, taught me a lot.

I mean compared to confronting a working class couple in their own home, pressuring them to buy something they can't afford and even if they could, they could manage without; standing on a stage singing at them must surely be easier…and more fun!

Mostly it was. However, on the occasions when you were singing your heart out, being ignored, the audience queuing at the bar with their backs to you, oblivious to your talent, and then, at the end of the evening, standing alongside you at the same bar while you waited for your money and had it counted out in full view, well, that was pretty tough.

There were a few times when I'd 'died' so badly I almost crept out the back door unpaid, avoiding the ritual humiliation. But I never did, it never came to that.

It was bad enough before the comedy crept in, when I was just a crooner, booked as 'bingo fodder', supplying 'musical wallpaper' while the customers queued, under your nose, for their next batch of tickets.

But as I was told many times by the senior pros... "Better than working, son, better than working!"

I felt I was moving onwards and upwards that summer, I was selling plenty of cleaners, £5 commission for each one, and getting lots of singing jobs at maybe £3 or £4 a night. I'd even bought my very first vehicle, a Ford 5 Hundredweight Van, (KWV 617, I'll never forget the number). At the same time, Mathews and Wright were rapidly expanding, they were all over South Yorkshire and the North Midlands like a rash.

They offered Ken the manager's job at their new shop in Chesterfield and he asked me if I'd like to join him as... wait for it...assistant manager.

It was a No Brainer, let's face it as, looking back, my employment CV thus far hadn't set the world alight... 'soggy bread' delivery boy, electrician without 'aptitude', and let's not dwell on the plumbing or even the radar.

Yes, this 'foot in the door' vacuum cleaner salesman would soon become a domestic appliance sales manager (alright, assistant).

So I relocated to north Derbyshire, to the town with the Crooked Spire (I'm avoiding any parallel with the description of the Spire and the activities of various vacuum cleaner salesman of the time).

I had a title, I was in management, even if the appointment involved sleeping on a mattress in a room over the shop. Heady with success, I sold my van and bought my first car, a Morris Minor Traveller OWT 476. She was a beauty, eggshell blue with mahogany woodwork and white trims around the wheel arches that looked fantastic. I later discovered they were there to hide the rust but, at the time, I was in dreamland.

Sadly the bubble was soon to burst, the Mathews and Wright empire was about to crumble. One day, alone in the shop, I had a call from head office telling me we were closed. A fleet of vans were on their way to remove the stock and I must lock the door and whitewash the windows which I did, much to the consternation of the landlord, who happened to pass by an hour later. He went pale and hurried off muttering "what about my rent".

All this meant that Ken and I were unemployed, but not to worry, we would go into business ourselves.

The following week, having fixed alternative accommodation, we set off from Chesterfield at the crack of dawn in OWT 476, heading for Cheetham Hill in Manchester which had hundreds of wholesale warehouses of every description. We'd fill the car with wildly diverse items to sell and be home in Chesterfield for a late breakfast. We'd then fill a suitcase each of what I can only describe as 'tat' and set off...on 'The Knocker'.

Among these items were (deep breath) PEGGY BASKETS! ONLY TWO SHILLINGS AND SIXPENCE!

"What you do, missus, is fill em full of pegs, clip em on the clothes line and slide em along, no more bending down to pick up the pegs."

"What's your favourite colour? Blue?"

"There you are then; I'll assemble it for you."

"Where's your pegs? Let's fill it up, clip it on the line, lovely. Only two and six, please."

"Thank you, good morning."

And exit left, with half crown in pocket and suitcase under arm!

Then as I reached the gate, I did a Lieutenant Columbo 360-degree turnaround.

"Before I go, show us your nails, luv."

"What a mess! Here, you need some pampering, luv. These nail clippers should be two and six as well, but seeing how you are already one of my favourite customers, to you…half price…one and threepence!"

And so it went on: peggy baskets, nail clippers, socks, underwear, rugs, even second-hand prams.

Not to mention the washing machine and vacuum cleaner repairs we were doing in our 'spare' time.

But the most comical direction we took was when we launched into made-to-measure men's suits. The Bradford Woollen Warehouse in Sheffield was run by the Swycher family, who were a big noise in the drapery business and the main attraction in dealing with them was that they gave us a rolling credit facility so we could stock our shops, (we had three by now) and offer our 'credit round' clients an extended range of goods.

These clients would pay us a fixed sum a week, say five shillings, and order what they wanted as long as the balance owing didn't exceed, say, twenty pounds.

We would call every week with our little black book, take their weekly payment and make sure their debt stayed towards the upper limit. It worked well, they could afford it and we had a profitable business and a healthy cashflow.

One of our regular calls was to a large terraced house in the town centre full of single foreign blokes, mainly of Italian and West Indian origin. The bosses at Bradford Woollen suggested we try made-to-measure suits; they would supply the cloth samples and teach us the measuring skills.

Amongst our first guinea pigs was a Mr Vespaniano and then there was Winston, whose surname we were never given. We didn't know if they were in the country legally and, frankly, didn't care.

We showed them our book of samples and they made their choices. Applying our new found skills, as instructed by the Bradford Woollen Tailor and with no small amount of bravado, we kicked off. Armed with our new tape measure, I called out the measurements and Ken wrote em down. We then took our deposits and bade them good day.

The following day we presented our calculations to the tailor.

I have to say that the materials they both chose were of very high quality, in Winston's case a shiny light grey mohair fabric.

The tailor pored over our measures for what seemed a long time,

"This Vespaniano chap, he's a big feller, isn't he?"

Ken and I looked at each other and concurred: "Yes, he was indeed a big feller."

"Okay, right."

"And how about this Winston bloke. Is he, er, how can I put it, is he… deformed?"

"No, he isn't."

"Well, gentlemen, according to these measurements I've got in front of me, he must be."

We exchanged worried glances, we couldn't possibly go back and re-measure, that would have revealed our (alright, my) incompetence.

So the tailor asked us to describe in detail Winston's physical appearance, making notes as he did, told us not to worry and to pick up the suits in a fortnight.

The day arrived and we arrived at the house.

Senor Vespaniano was first and to our immense relief the suit fitted him, not like a glove but it was a reasonable fit and he was well pleased.

Now it was Winston's turn, he was a laid back West Indian guy, almost six feet tall and very, very thin. We put the suit on him, and… he disappeared!

I swear it, he turned round twice and the suit never moved!

"Man," came a voice from within the folds of cloth, "there's plenty of room in here, Man."

(Every now and then in life, people are capable of surmounting obstacles, achieving things, solving problems and getting out of trouble. Quite often this is when they are in a desperate or embarrassing situation. Something comes to their aid, they find an extra dimension).

Then I heard myself say…

"You're a lucky feller, there, Winston, you are now wearing the new Drape."

"Really."

"Yep, you're ahead of the game, Winston, with this new Drape."

I motioned him to the mirror, gathering a handful of mohair together behind his back.

"Wow, nice!" (him not me).

Another pair of satisfied customers, then.

Funny what you could get away with in those days. I suppose people were more trusting, not as worldly and less cynical.

We weren't conning people; we were providing a service they needed and mostly giving value for money. Our shortcomings were revealed by our over enthusiasm and our belief that we could succeed at almost anything.

However, the tailoring adventure was a step too far and wasn't repeated.

We continued our diverse operations, which included a Ladies Fashion Shop, a Credit Drapery Round, and a Domestic Appliance Sales and Repair Business.

We never had any money, constantly robbing Peter to pay Paul and only able to continue by the extended credit offered by Bradford Woollen. Then I had a phone call from Dennis Swycher, telling me he needed us in his office…TODAY!

We trooped in wearing our gents tailors' clothes, our mechanics overalls having been discarded in the van.

Mr Swycher lounged behind an enormous polished top mahogany desk. The desktop was completely empty of any office accoutrements but as he motioned us to sit down, a phone rang, he slid out a drawer, picked up the phone, said a few words, put the phone back in the drawer and slid it shut. Very impressive!

A secretary appeared noiselessly from behind us, slid a folder in front of him and left in complete silence. Very unnerving!

Still mute, he flipped open the folder, pursing his lips. The silence was broken by his long low whistle. Pure theatre!

But we weren't enjoying the show one bit.

"According to these figures, gentlemen, your debt to Bradford Woollen has spiralled out of control, as I speak, there is £920 due immediately; it's been building during the last three months due to you ignoring our statements and then a further £1,500 due in a fortnight."

I exchanged furtive looks with Ken. 920 quid? We hadn't got £90, never mind the rest. (As I write today, £900 doesn't seem a lot, but fifty years ago it was a year's wages and could even buy you a small house).

Denis drummed his fingers on the desk. "I'll take PDs," he said.

Ken knew and to prove it he produced a bookful from his pocket: Post Dated Cheques!

Ken dutifully wrote out a fistful at £50 a week until he ran out of cheques. Of course, the writing was on the wall. Apart from the possibility that some of these PDs were likely to bounce, our account was closed, so no more supplies. We were in a hole.

We had a number of projects on the go but none of them were financially viable and we had no capital whatsoever, relying purely on intermittent cash flow.

There followed a period of financial hardship I wouldn't like to experience again. Before long we were on first name terms with most of the bailiffs and debt collecting agencies in the area.

We owed thousands and we hadn't got a bean.

Sacrifices had to be made, I remember the dark day when Ken had his beloved gleaming Ford Consul repossessed. Then my pride and joy, the Morris Minor Traveller, was swapped for a Ford Thames Van ODJ 764, which itself became a target for the 'Repo' men, resulting in us having to park it in a side street up to a mile away from home every night and do the rest on foot whatever the weather.

We ultimately had to close our "flagship' dress shop and as me and Madge were living literally above the shop, with our new baby, Stephen, it meant us moving into Ken and Lily's front bedroom.

They had two girls, Linda and Carol, and we all squeezed into their three-bedroomed semi.

For the first few months of his life, our new-born Stephen was a nightmare, screaming night after night. Nobody slept and we were all at the end of our tether when we heard of a caravan for sale,£100 and only a fiver down, I gave the man the fiver and bought it unseen.

I went down to the local caravan site and arranged a pitch: we were on our way!

Not so fast, the transporter driver returned to say that the farmer whose land the caravan was on wouldn't release it due to unpaid ground rent.

Off went the seller in his Land Rover, vowing to 'sort it'.

I don't know how but, two hours later, he turned up towing a 22ft, somewhat tatty, caravan. We parked it on some waste ground by our workshop and I spent the weekend painting it…eggshell blue! Okay, wouldn't have been my first choice but it was a job lot from the local shop that was going cheap.

We towed it to the site, coupled up the water and electrics and moved in to our very first (admittedly mobile) home.

Hard to say how we survived that period. The caravan had to be paid off at a pound a week and every Monday a lady would call, many's the time when my wife Madge hadn't got a quid on her and, on seeing the lady's approach, would lie down on the floor to escape detection.

Later on, when she was very pregnant with our number two child Michele, she felt very vulnerable, convinced that the bump could be seen through the window. It took almost three years to pay off that hundred pounds. I've still got the payment card, a stark reminder of how desperate things were.

Somehow we scraped through, working all hours, plus

I started to find regular work on the club circuit, strictly as a singer but always wanting to make the move into comedy, yet lacking the confidence to make the jump.

There were many comedians to look up to back then. There were the obvious stars like Tommy Cooper and Ken Dodd, but I was inspired by a local 'legend'. Ronnie Dukes was the most successful club act of his time and with his wife Rickie Lee sold out wherever they appeared.

Ronnie was a roly-poly figure of a man, a real bundle of energy. He could sing, dance and his gravelly-voiced delivery was devastating. Much of his comedy was aimed at his mother-in-law, who played piano in the act. With his own band live on stage, he would just take over the place.

I used to watch him tear audiences apart and wonder if one day that could be me getting that reaction.

Instead, I was pussy-footing around, relying on my singing to get me through and only dipping my toe in the comedy pond when I was faced with an 'easy' audience.

So much so, that I developed an 'on-stage' split personality. Let's say that in the northern half of my area – Barnsley/Sheffield, where they were harder to please – I would be a crooner of popular songs with a nice line in chat; whereas in Derbyshire and Nottinghamshire, where they were generally more forgiving, I would sing a bit, do a few gags and, later in the evening, launch into a full-blown comedy routine.

But imagine how the Notts and Derbys club-goers used to feel when, after taking a 20/30 mile trip north to watch me, they'd find a totally different animal. They'd be confused, I guess.

IN AT THE DEEP END

I was thrown in at the deep end almost by accident. I regularly worked my local club in Newbold, in Chesterfield, where they loved my comedy.

The drummer, Paul Derek, told me he was part of a Thalidomide Charity Road Show and would I fancy doing a few dates with them. I jumped at the chance and a few weeks later turned up for my first show to discover I was billed as the main comedian. The organisers, Brian and Eunice Hartley, themselves parents of a Thalidomide son, had taken Paul's praising of me literally, so I had no option but to put the comedy first.

The shows were always sold out with five or six artistes (we used to be 'turns') performing and were a great vehicle for me, ''the comic'.

The added bonus was that, after the show, I would usually be rebooked at the venue, plus perhaps several surrounding clubs, as...a comedian!

No turning back, then, and my fame was beginning to spread.

The local club magazines were very complimentary about the 'New Comedy Sensation who Sings as Well' and I was on my way.

There were a few hiccups here and there; one in particular springs to mind after I answered an advertisement for a Granada TV Talent Show who were looking for singers. At my audition I discovered the producer, Rod Taylor, lounging back in his chair.

The conversation went something like (and I've never let Rod forget this)…

HE: "So what are you going to sing for me?"

ME: (nervously) "The Twelfth of Never."

HE: (with heavy irony) "Hotly followed by what?"

To be fair to Rod, I was the 43rd 'wanabee' through his door that day, so he could be forgiven his somewhat jaundiced attitude.

No comments were made at the end of my audition and I was soon 'hotly' out the door. Arriving home two or three hours later, I got a phone call from Granada telling me I'd passed the audition and..."would you please report to the studio for the recording tomorrow".

I was in a real sweat, my first appearance on television and no time to rehearse.

The following day, I was ushered into the studio having given my music to the bandleader, Derek Hilton. I was stood on a mark and when I asked the floor manager what I should do, he said:

"Just follow the camera with the red light on and you'll be fine".

The intro started and I began 'The Twelfth of Never', craning my neck to see which camera lit up as they circled around me like a shoal of predatory sharks, at least that's how it felt, way out of my comfort zone. I was intimidated, to put it mildly.

A few nights later it went out, and there I was for all the world to see, caught, like a rabbit in the headlights, paralysed with fear, my eyes woodenly following the camera as instructed.

The following week the local clubland magazine carried the headline: 'KEEP OFF THE TELLY, BERNIE'.

The article then went on to give an accurate description of my TV maiden performance (kinder to say 'debut'), suggesting it could have finished my career before it had started.

True to say, the offers hardly rolled in but not enough

people had watched it to make any difference to me apart from the emotional scarring (and there'd be plenty more of that to come).

Slowly but surely my clubland reputation was spreading and I started to appear in prestigious gala and 'command' shows, as they were called, where the best acts in clubland were billed.

I was still singing, but comedy was now my strongest card, involving a few madcap impressions and one or two small props.

How I wish I had a video of my Sixties act...but there were no recording facilities available back then. How embarrassing would it be?

CHAPTER 8
ON THE ROAD TO STARDOM?

As the Sixties rolled on, our family grew. In 1965, our third child Tracy was born, and by now we had fought our way out of the trailer park and had moved into a three-bedroomed semi on the edge of town. It was blindingly obvious where my future lay and it was to our mutual advantage for me and Ken to go our separate ways, so we divided up the business, with me retaining the shop in Chesterfield town centre. With a manager in place, this gave me the freedom to work further and further afield doing what I do best.

But even though I was on the road more often, I was still, like many of my contemporaries, a 'semi pro'. I remember being told by Brian Barber, an act from Doncaster, that he was about to become a full-time professional, or, as he put it, "I'm going on the boards". I had no idea what Brian was talking about. At the time, it was akin to being launched into space.

However, my life was about to change when I was put

in touch with Anthony Bygraves, son of the legendary Max.

Anthony produced and appeared in a Summer Season Revue at the Babbacombe Theatre, Torquay. The previous summer the Welsh comedian Bryn Phillips had appeared there and Anthony was looking for a Northern club comedian to take his place.

He came to see me work at the Intake Sports and Social Club in Doncaster and liked what he saw.

No preamble from our Anthony: "26 weeks starting in May, £55 a week, non-negotiable".

Who was I to negotiate? I was just a 'turn', a comedian who could sing a bit or, if you like, a singer who could 'comedy' a bit!

In modern parlance, it was a 'no brainer', my chance to move into theatres. The club circuit was lucrative, with regular work while living at home but at the time the club acts were seen as outsiders to the show business 'Powers that Be'.

As I saw it, this was my chance. I would be in show business proper and, obviously, working with Anthony in Babbacombe whilst his Dad, Max, was in a summer show next door in Torquay was an opportunity to be 'noticed'.

Would it turn out like this? To find out, I had to get there.

With three children under the age of seven, renting a house or a cottage for the season was out of the question, not on 55 quid a week. And so, a caravan it was.

This time, a touring model, a Willerby Sprite, 22ft long, in good condition and all for £125.

I'd already splurged out on a lovely big car, a 1964 silver grey Jaguar Mark 10, CUT 322B (you didn't think I'd forget that number, did you?). £10 was all it took for a tow bar to be fitted and we were ready for off.

Loading the caravan with five months' supplies was hysterical: how I wish I had a video of that epic!

But loaded we were, to the 'gunnels' (whatever that means), and off I drove, a first-time caravan puller, the scourge of motorists everywhere, swanning along at a steady 40mph, a clear open road ahead, not a sign of another vehicle. (That's because they're all behind me, trying vainly to overtake).

It couldn't have been easy, overtaking this particular 'Road Train'. The Jag was at least 18 feet long, plus four foot of tow bar, then 22 feet of Willerby. But I didn't care; I was off on a big adventure.

Never one to miss a chance of earning a few quid, though, I'd taken a job in a social club in Nottingham 'while I was passing'.

The money was important, I was not going to earn a lot for the next five months and the extra would come in handy. What a sight we must have presented as we trundled into the club car park.

I wound down the caravan legs, Madge put the kids to bed (they absolutely loved it), while I went indoors and did what I did best.

I can't recall much about the show but I do remember the following morning heading south with not a lot of sleep under my belt.

To borrow the quote from a decade earlier, "It Wor a Beautiful May Morning" all over again.

A lot had happened in that decade and I don't just mean the Beatles. I was married with a young family and was no longer just a 'turn'. I was on my way to becoming a variety artiste, a theatre entertainer no less, (albeit for 55 quid a week).

With few motorways in 1969, my journey south took me on the A38, right through Birmingham city centre in the morning rush hour.

How those Brummies loved me, as I completed lap after lap of the famous Bull Ring, swopping lanes, ignoring the shouts as I looked for a sign that said: A38 South for Fame and Fortune.

By the time we'd reached the M5 south of Bromsgrove, I had started to relax, as the worst was surely over. Which is when it started raining, not just rain lashing down but the most spectacular thunderstorm in living memory.

I slowed to about 40mph and was just about keeping the Juggernaut straight when…KERRASH!!!

The biggest bang came from the back of the car, which slewed violently as I fought to keep control. I ground to a halt on the hard shoulder and as I looked in the mirror I could see that the caravan window was tilting at a crazy angle.

"OH, NO! THE CARAVAN WHEEL'S PUNCTURED AND I HAVEN'T GOT A SPARE."

I put the hazards on and stepped out into the monsoon to inspect the damage. Within seconds I was soaked to the skin and then it got much, much worse. It wasn't a puncture, nothing so simple.

The bolts that attached the wheel to the hub had sheared, with the result that the wheel had almost disappeared up into the interior of the van, which was resting on what was left of the hub.

Fortunately we were all okay, although the kids seemed unperturbed, perhaps they were too young to appreciate the situation.

The police turned up within minutes; perhaps they'd been trailing me, following an 'Accident waiting to Happen'.

They coned off the area, helped me to uncouple the caravan and leaving it, like some kind of beached whale, escorted me down to Strensham Services.

"Where you heading?," they said.

"Torquay, have to be there first thing in the morning for me summer season rehearsals."

Quizzical looks from one to the other. No, they didn't know who the hell I was, and I was in no mood to enlighten them.

"Give you a tip, son, don't call the Emergency Services, they'll charge you an arm and a leg just to get you off the motorway. Make your way out of the back of the Service Area."

(Those were the days when you could actually do that).

"Head towards Tewkesbury, about a mile down the road there's a Garage; they might be able to help you."

Ten minutes later, the Jag rolled to a halt in front of a rundown workshop, it was like a visit to 'The Land that Time Forgot'. The two blokes who eyed me up and down were father and son. I'd interrupted their tea break but they didn't seem too bothered, perhaps I'd made their day. There was the car, a Mark 10 Jag, pretty rare and there was me, the driver, fully clothed and I'd been swimming.

The predicament was explained. I had to be in Devon by the morning and I had a very sick caravan leaning on the tarmac up the road.

So what did they do? They only shut up shop, locked up the garage and followed me up to the scene to see what could be done.

They then spent the rest of the day chasing round

Cheltenham and Gloucester to various scrap yards and caravan dealers to get me a new hub and a second-hand wheel to fit it.

The accident happened late morning and it was almost 7pm when I followed them into the Service Area, fully hooked up and roadworthy.

"How much do I owe you ," I said.

"Well, the hub cost us three and the second-hand wheel was a couple of quid, then there's our time...erm, is 12 Quid alright?"

"Twelve quid?" I asked incredulously.

Seriously, can you believe those two blokes did all that, closing down their business so they could get me mobile again, covering half the county hunting down the parts, spending the whole day getting us going, and all for twelve quid?

The Angels were smiling down on us that day.

Do you know, it's well over 40 years since that never-to-be-forgotten day, and since then I must have passed the spot hundreds of times, but I never found the time to seek them out, remind them of their generosity and thank them properly. I'm really sorry I didn't.

I can't even remember their names. And that's really sad!

Of course the trek wasn't over by any means. I drove through the whole of that night, arriving exhausted as dawn broke on the outskirts of Teignmouth and for the first time in almost twelve hours I heard a little voice pipe up from the back seat: "Can we see the sea yet?"

I parked in the middle of a deserted farmer's field that had a sign on the gate that said 'Caravans', wound the legs down and two hours later uncoupled the car, said to Madge "I'll leave you to it'" and drove off to rehearsals.

I was determined not to be late. I suppose I was so aware of being an outsider, the 'Northern Club Act', moving into unknown territory, that I wasn't going to let anyone think I wasn't serious.

Rehearsals were fine, the company – about twelve in number – were a great bunch and after a productive morning we broke for lunch at the local restaurant. Still on my best behaviour, I was okay until I had an 'apple pie' incident . The apple hadn't been prepared properly and the husk from the pip became detached from the slice and became attached, almost like a suction pad, to the rear of my tongue.

At first I carried on, trying to dislodge it by drinking but it wouldn't move. I still tried to act normally but eventually my eyes started to water, my nose was running, I started to gag prior to going into a full-scale choking fit.

Pandemonium ensued, the worst thing from my point of view wasn't the fact that I might choke to death. No, it was the embarrassment Factor.

How weird is that? I may have been northern but by eck I hadn't forgotten I was English.

I recovered, finished the day's rehearsals and eventually returned to the field where I'd left the caravan that morning. It was gone!

Keep calm, Bernard, it turned out it had been relocated by the farmer.

A few days later, we found a lovely site over the river in Shaldon and within a week or two, life assumed some kind of normality.

The show had opened and was going really well from my point of view. Now would the gamble pay off? After all, I'd uprooted my wife Madge and three kids from the comfort of our three-bedroom semi to spend five months in a caravan in deepest Devon. If we'd had a cat, there wouldn't have been room to swing it. Conditions were, shall we say, cramped. But we managed, even had friends and family come to stay during the summer (how mad was that?).

But career wise, would it be worth it? Anthony's Dad, the legendary Max Bygraves, came to see the show and he popped round backstage afterwards and was very complimentary about my performance. A few days later, I got a call from his manager Jock Jacobson, inviting me to sign with his agency.

I was thrilled: it really looked as if things were going according to plan. The word on the street in northern clubland was that to 'make it', you had to have a London agent. Without one, you were forever on the outside looking in. It was 'us and them'.

With a London agent you could enter another world, the real world of show business. The world where the power brokers, the TV producers, the star makers and everybody who was anybody, met and eat together and did the deals that could make you a star.

Looking back to the Sixties, it's clear how big the gulf was between the clubs of the north and the world of theatre and television. A few years would pass before Johnny Hamp would weave his magic and show the world what the northern clubs had to offer with 'The Comedians' on ITV but, back then, London was were the deals were done. And I was in!

Within a few weeks, I got another call from Jock asking me if I fancied a tour of South Africa the following winter as part of the Max Bygraves Show. Needless to say I accepted. South Africa was a great experience for me, but I have to admit I was ill equipped to entertain the theatre audiences over there. Coming as I did from the club circuit, my act was not tailored for the more sophisticated following that Max attracted.

Thankfully I wasn't too exposed, being just a small part of a terrific variety bill. My job was to do a short spot and compere the first half which featured Rostall and Schaeffer playing classical piano (in fact they had one each); the soprano Gillian Humphries; and finally the Freelanders, a folk group from the North East. We got on famously and enjoyed some great times, especially in Cape Town. Clifton Beach being one of our favourite haunts. The tour was a world away from what I was used to but I was young and eager to learn.

While I was over there, I got a telegram from my agent telling me I'd been offered a summer season in Jersey which, after a call home to a now heavily-pregnant Madge, I decided to take. It surely was the right move for an ambitious young entertainer like me.

CHAPTER 9
THE SEVENTIES

That decision to take the Jersey summer season offer was life changing. As with Babbacombe the previous year, it was taken for all the right reasons, taking me into the world of show business PROPER.

I still had my cherished Mark 10 Jag and I remember phoning the Jersey producer Dick Ray (later to become my manager), if the roads on the island were wide enough to take my car. He must have thought I was mad: "Of course they are, I drive a Mark 10 too". Recalling that tale makes it clear how little I knew about the world outside of my comfort zone.

Timing is everything, though, and in May 1970, I knew I'd got it wrong. I was leaving my family behind at the worst possible time. David was born on the day after my birthday, April 23rd. Madge, bless her, always supportive, said: "Off you go, see you in a few weeks".

I headed south feeling pretty wretched, homesick already (remember no mobile phones or Skype, the only way to keep in touch was queuing at a phone box with a pocket full of coins) and as I followed that long bonnet onto the ferry in Weymouth, I wondered if I was making a big mistake.

No going back, I told myself as I drove ashore onto the island that would play an important part in my career during the next few years.

I was performing, nay starring, (don't get excited, read on) in the touring 'Excitement Show' that entertained the residents at different hotels every week. Six nights, twelve hotels (you do the maths!)

The show was made up of four dancers; a double guitar act who also provided the musical backing; a 'Soubrette' (look it up), namely Dick's wife Peggy and the 'Top of the Bill', yours truly.

This is how it worked, we'd turn up at the first hotel, pile into the kitchen and get changed into our stage gear. Boys and girls altogether, modesty at a minimum (hopefully the evening meal had been over long enough for the hotplates to have cooled down!)

All the hotels had a ballroom, the floor would be cleared and the show would start, with the running order something like....Band (both of them) Overture; Girls: Me, doing the Warm-up; Peggy Ray: Band (still only two); Me; Finale, with everybody on (60 minutes in all).

Then quick, but really quick, pile back into the kitchen, pack up, back in the cars, roar round to the next hotel and repeat the previous procedure. For twenty weeks! What the hell, I was in show business.

Although the company was great and I forged some lifelong friendships that summer, I was really missing my family especially my new-born. So I broke the rules. My contract stipulated that I could not leave the island during the run of the show.

There was a reason for this clause. Jersey was prone to sea fog rolling in and closing down the airport so if you were on the mainland when this occurred, you'd be a 'no show' person and in our business, there's no such thing, as 'The show must go on'.

Who said that first, I wonder? Whoever it was, I bet he wasn't kicking his heels on an island, had got a night off and was missing his kids.

So without telling Dickie, I jumped on a plane. I figured if I asked him he might say no and I wouldn't blame him. I mean, a sea fret slides in from Guernsey and before you know it, the 'excitement' levels in the 'Excitement Show' are looking vulnerable without the top of the bill, 'Mr Excitement' himself.

Imagine the headlines: "Excitement Dented", "Dick Ray Demented", "Top Turn Absented"

So I never told him.

I was met that Saturday morning at East Midlands Airport and rolled up at 41 Glenfield Crescent as a BIG surprise, having decided to tell no one in case of a weather glitch.

But to cradle our tiny baby, albeit briefly, was worth it.

It was lovely having that day at home but all too soon I was southbound on the Vickers Viscount, breathing a sigh of relief as we touched down at St Helier.

The whole 24 hours had been overshadowed by worrying about the weather.

Yes, I'd been a naughty boy but had got away with it.

IN THE SUMMERTIME

Those Jersey summers were different, there was a great 'company' feel about our time there, perhaps because we were 'stuck' in a sense on the island. Leaving, even for a day, was frowned upon as I explained earlier and that helped people to bond as a group.

I remember the 'in-house' language that sprung up. Going to the beach became 'Beachingtons', shopping was 'Shoppingtons' and some people were given titles they haven't lost to this day.

If your name was Stan, you'd be 'Stan The Man'.

Trev our drummer (yes, him with the artificial leg) became 'Trev The Rev'.

Saxophonist Jim was 'Jim The Flute' and our roadie Bob, who loved to lie in until lunchtime, became 'Bob The Bed'.

Bob and I still swop Christmas cards but if you held a gun to my head, five decades later, I couldn't tell you his surname.

I know Bob met Max during that Jersey summer. Max, short for Maxine (and a basketball player) was a waitress in the cafe opposite our rehearsal room, and they subsequently married, raised a family and live on the south coast. A really sweet story, I was there and saw it happen.

The other thing we all had in common was energy. After two shows a night, we would decide on a 'party house', visit the Co-op Bakery and laden with armfuls of fresh, still hot baguettes, would spend hours enjoying cheese, wine and, wait for it, MONOPOLY!

Yes, we played Monopoly, all night long: ROCK AND ROLL!

During one party, which was overrunning somewhat, as dawn was breaking we spotted the Weymouth ferry passing the headland, shortly to berth in St Helier.

No further ado, we jumped in our cars, roared down to

the cafe on the harbour and gorged ourselves on bacon butties as we watched the passengers stream ashore. Then home, a few hours' kip and two shows that night.

If anyone offered me that scenario now! I'm exhausted just thinking about it.

Things changed dramatically with the arrival of the school holidays, and not a moment too soon, as the 'party animals', those Monopoly maestros, put on their alter egos, becoming responsible parents as whole families descended for a long summer break.

It was idyllic, we had the days to ourselves apart from the charity cricket matches and the regular summer fetes to open, which were always fun.

We were also in a nice vein of work, too, as holiday audiences were always in the mood to be entertained, a far cry from our usual habitats in northern clubland, but it wouldn't be long before the real world beckoned.

I still recall the farewells as the holidays ended. In those days security was lax and as a non-passenger, I carried my infant son across the tarmac to the Viscount steps and as his three elder siblings excitedly tumbled aboard, tearfully handed him over to Madge. I watched the plane take off and disappear into the sunset and felt very, very alone.

The "see you in a few weeks" had a hollow ring about it.

I've often thought in later years about long goodbyes and believe the one doing the travelling (usually me) had the best of it, moving into different worlds with plenty of new people and challenges to meet.

Whereas the one left behind (the missus) had the silent house and the mundane, same old lifestyle to cope with.

How many times have I been there, the early morning

pick-up, tearful hugs, long drive to the airport, every step taking you further away from the people you loved.

Then perhaps 24 hours later, stepping aboard the QE2 for a three-week cruise around the South Pacific. So who got the best deal? What a no brainer!

Years ago, I was in pro digs with a couple more comics, one of whom had his wife with him. She was ironing his shirt for that night's performance. We, the lads, were having a great time laughing and talking about the show when she paused with the ironing, looked at us and said: "It's alright for you lot, but what about the wives, we only get what's left."

What a telling phrase that is: "We only get what's left". It sums it up perfectly.

The comedians (especially the comedians) are always the first to tell you how tough it can be getting laughs from an unwilling crowd, then enthusing over the great night they've just had (virtually having had a love affair with a room full of strangers).

The adrenaline rush we get during a show is very rewarding and can be addictive, but when the performance ends, the 'high' is followed by a vacuum, often filled by drinking or gambling or other forms of extreme behaviour. The next stage might be exhaustion and when that sequence of events has concluded, the partner..."only gets what's left".

Autumn had arrived and the Mark 10 nose was pointing north, the island and Weymouth, were receding in the distance, so what next? The clubs, of course!

I was always working, so I must have been doing something right and there were so many opportunities to get a strong, copper-bottomed act together that would survive anywhere. I'd introduced some props to my act and I was different. I got a kick out of picking up things that were lying around the stage and making something happen.

I was in a club (Ilkeston Co-op since you've asked) and at the end of my last spot, they asked me if I would come back on stage to "draw t'raffle".

The tickets were in two large biscuit tins, about a foot deep. I drew out the tickets then jumped in the tins, doing a 'Bolero' around the stage. It got such a big laugh, the following day I went round the back of my local supermarket and there they were piled as high as the eye could see, comedy gold! (alright, tin).

The manager said: "Take as many as you want, we're only going to scrap em".

So I did, calling regularly to restock, that 'bloke wot dances wi' tins on his feet'.

Here's a bit of hindsight: today a biscuit tin of that vintage in good condition is worth upwards of 50 quid.

Ooh, If only? I could have had them, by the hundreds, kept them somewhere warm and dry, took a few to the auction every now and then…what a pension plan that would have been! Clearly, I never did!

1971 was looking good, I'd been invited to appear in the annual Yorkshire 'Clubland Command Show', which was a real feather in my cap. The artistes invited were considered to be the pick of the current crop of 'turns' and, even better, the venue was the internationally famous Batley Variety Club.

To appear on the Batley Stage gave you proper clout. It meant you were on your way, climbing the ladder out of the smaller club circuit into the world of Major League Cabaret, rubbing shoulders with the biggest stars in the world. That's no exaggeration, as Shirley Bassey, Louis Armstrong, Neil Sedaka had all appeared there.

It was The Mecca of Clubland and I was there.

The night came, I did my spot and if I say so myself, it as a riot (biscuit tins especially). The manager, Derek Smith, came backstage and said: "Where have you sprung from," then "follow me, somebody wants to meet you".

"Who's that?"

"Barney Colehan, that's who".

Barney was the producer of 'The Good Old Days', the BBC flagship show which was recorded in front of an audience dressed in Edwardian Gear at the City Varieties Theatre in Leeds.

Barney was seated at a table full of people and, to have a conversation and avoid blocking peoples' view of the on-stage proceedings, I had to kneel at his feet. Very appropriate, I thought, because to appear on the 'Good Old Days' I would have prostrated myself and licked his boots.

"Where have you sprung from?" (They're all saying that).

That was it in a nutshell, the gulf between the social club circuit, where hundreds of us were toiling away, and the TV world, was enormous. You could bum around for years without being heard of until, if you were in the right place at the right time, you might get lucky. And I was and I had got a break.

It took a few months for things to click into place but in October 1971 I turned up at the iconic City Varieties for my first 'proper' TV appearance.

The theatre, compared to the clubs I was used to, was a dream venue. Alongside me as roadie and confidence booster was Mick Norcliffe, a Leeds lad who I'd played rugby with in the RAF. Mick was centre to my wing and if you know your rugby, a winger is only as good as the service he gets and I'd got the best from Mick, who only gave me the ball when I had a chance to run with it, no 'hospital' passes.

We'd kept in touch after demob and there we were, hoping to score in a very different world.

Barney had been very helpful in making sure I'd be 'alright on the night' and together we'd put together a tight five-minute patter spot ending with a classic comic song from the era entitled…wait for it…"I'm goin' back to Imazaz, Im as Has a Pub next door'.

Everything in the show was in the style of the Edwardian Music Hall.

The audience played their part, dressed to the nines, some of them even sporting false beards and moustaches (and that was just the women).

The performers, their clothes and the material they used, had to be so authentic. It was a real blast from the past and very successful for its time.

Barney gave me a lovely build-up and I was on. The audience were terrific and I came off bathed in sweat but well pleased.

Topping the bill was someone who would become a national treasure, Les Dawson. Les, well known for his down-to-earth lugubrious style, was much loved and went down a storm. I felt I'd played my part of a very successful show.

However, in the bar afterwards, Les took the wind out of my sails.

"You're alright but you're only doing the same stuff as a hundred other comics".

(I have since worked out he'd seen something in me and was trying to help).

"Why don't you find your own direction?"

"How do you mean?"

"What kind of comedy do you really enjoy?"

"Well, I love mucking about with props."

"Well, why don't you go out and become a 'props' comic. Nobody else is doing it, go on, be original."

All this advice was given in a kind tone by a man who was revered even back then as a legend. I'll always be so grateful to Les for taking time to speak to me. There were many more important people in the bar that night clamouring for his attention but that few minutes alone with him inspired me and gave me the kick up the backside I needed.

His words gave me something to think about. I loved the nonsense I got from the visual elements in my act, the biscuit tins were a prime example, so why not follow his advice?

The following day (and it WAS the day after), fate decided to smile on me. I was walking through Chesterfield when I passed a charity shop with a sign in the window: 'Everything you see is 50p'. There, looking at me, was the head of a lion, a full-sized lionskin hearth rug.

A few pages ago, I used the phrase 'see how things have moved on'. When I look at that lion skin now, I see the tragedy behind it. A magnificent animal was shot so that some wealthy Victorian could adorn his fireside. What an appalling thought. But 50 years ago I was looking at a comedy prop, nothing else. So I bought it, for 50p.

It became part of a growing arsenal: the tins, various hats, a 'trick' mike stand and now the lion. I would try to follow Les's advice to the letter. I'd become a 'prop' comic.

The 'Good Old Days' was shown the following March on BBC 1 and in the meantime I'd had further good news.

The TV Show was going live. The 'Beeb' had joined forces with the Delfont organisation and a stage version of the show was going to Blackpool for the summer. And I was in it!

Twelve months earlier this 'turn' was working the local clubs and now he was off to Blackpool to appear in the number one summer season. Heady times indeed.

The venue was the Winter Gardens Pavilion Theatre and the producer was the number one Delfont producer, Dickie Hurran. He'd seen me compere a Sunday concert at the Coventry Belgrade Theatre, starring Buddy Greco, and liked what he saw.

He took me to lunch in London and filled me in on my involvement, not only would I have my own five-minute spot but I would take part in production numbers, singing AND dancing at the same time.

I was bottom of the bill (so far down the poster I saw a dog pointing at my name with his back leg) but it didn't matter, look at the company I was keeping.

Here's the bill: Ronnie Ronalde, the singer/yodeller who'd enjoyed a stream of hits in the 50's; 'Two Ton' Tessie O Shea, larger than life, wielding a ukelele; Ben Warriss, one half of Jewell and Warriss, as big in their day as Morecambe and Wise would be years later; Joe Church, a seasoned comic with a lovely gentle style; Tony Cawley, experienced Irish comedian with material to die for; Rod Hull (yes, him) and Emu; Rob Murray, (my favourite), a laconic Australian juggler with a line of patter that always creased me; and 'The Company', a 20-strong team of boys and girls, singers and dancers all; and finally me, plucked from the clubs. Only way was up!

The stage manager was Frank Woodruff who, now and again, was tough on me. It was all about timing: my solo spot in the first half was set at 5 minutes; not a second more, not a second less. As a club act, the clock was never an issue, you'd do your allotted time and run over if you were going well, (unless that impinged on the great God of Bingo, then heaven help you!) But in the world of theatre it was very different. Every night as I came off I passed him in the corner to hear my timing: "5 minutes 45 seconds, Mr Clifton, will you please stick to your timing, if every one did an extra 45 seconds we'd run into overtime."

"Sorry, Frank"; or

"4 minutes 30 seconds, Mr Clifton, remember other artistes are on a quick change and there's a scene change happening behind you, so by not doing your time, you are putting colleagues under pressure."

"Sorry, Frank."

He was right of course, it was a discipline that was new to me, so I had to learn.

Subsequently it felt good to hear: "5 minutes 5 seconds, Mr Clifton, Thank you very much."

The summer rolled on and I mixed with the stars at various events, football and cricket matches, garden fetes, etc. I was a lowly member of the show biz fraternity (often the only one I'd never heard of), but I was still in the swim and it felt good.

There was talk of the show transferring to the West End in the autumn, which would have been fantastic, but sadly Mr. Hurran called us all into a meeting to tell us that wasn't going to happen.

We were all very disappointed but after he'd delivered the news, the silence was broken by a tired, unmistakably Australian voice: who else but 'Juggler Murray'.

"Dickie, if it'll help, we'll all take a pay cut".

Hysterical! The whole room went into 'silent corpse'.

FOR YOUR ENTERTAINMENT—

Bernie Clifton
COMEDY & SONG

92 *Riverdale Park*
Lowgates
Staveley, nr. Chesterfield

TELEPHONES :
CHESTERFIELD 75998
STAVELEY 669

A young man going places, but still living in a caravan

You wouldn't get me up in one of those!

My stage suit. Can't see the bike clips!

Bob Hope – old buddies

Me, Tony Selby and Parky. Why? It's a secret!

Having the best of times with Stuart Gillies

That moment! That smile

A proper end of the Pier Show, along with Doddy,
there's nowhere I'd rather be

Look at me with hair!

Half man, half mad

Marathon? Just the one, perhaps

On a wing and a prayer

Tidy for the year (I mean the car)

And now for the Lap of Honour

Tracy won a prize for the best hair

My mentor, Les Dawson. He put me right!

Two St Helen's lads getting a grip

With Joe Pasquale. The stalls are alive to the sound of laughter

With 'The Govner', and lady Dodd

The most bizarre thing to say: speaking on behalf of us all, without asking.

I've never forgotten the moment, not just what Rob said but the way he said it.

It's my enduring memory of such a funny character.

The season ended, not a riotous success for me but great experience nevertheless, so what next? The clubs, of course. Apart from working non-stop around the country over the winter, both in social clubs and cabaret, Derek Smith was booking me for a series of month-long stints as compere at Batley Variety Club, a great gig: on to do a short warm-up, introduce a couple of acts then close the first half (best time to go on) with a 20-minute spot. Following the interval, I did a presentation spot, handing out flowers, etc, to people celebrating a special event.

And then as the club darkened, a drum roll and in my best compere's voice:

"Ladies and gentlemen, Batley Variety Club is proud to present, live on stage...

"MR NEIL SEDAKA" or "DANNY LA RUE AND COMPANY" or "TOM JONES".

What a place to be, in the middle of it all, sharing the stage with these legends!

Neil Sedaka was a revelation, he would run through all his hits, from the poignant ballads, 'Hungry Years' and 'Solitaire', where he'd have them eating out of his hand; then he'd ring the changes, go up tempo with a rock and roll medley. Without any announcements, he'd leave the stage before returning for an encore. (I'd be in the wings with my coat on ready to get out the back door and beat the traffic), but I never missed his encore.

Just when you thought there were no more buttons he

could press, he'd come back, sit at the piano and start softly singing his 'Betty Grable' song. What a finish!

He could take an audience anywhere he wanted. After lifting the roof off, he brought the atmosphere down to almost a recital feel with that beautiful song about his childhood, 'Crush'. Genius!

The one star I never got to introduce was Shirley Bassey, as she had other ideas. Fifteen minutes before the interval ended, all the bars closed, (no serving whilst Ms B was on) then, with 5 minutes remaining, the lights began to dim, very gradually at first, until the auditorium was in cabaret 'state', the house music faded and there we were, an expectant silence, a goose-bumping quiet, very eerie.

A boisterous late night cabaret scene had been turned on it's head as 1,500 people held their collective breath, and then, in the hush...she came on!

Wearing a fantastic, shimmering gold full-length gown, she just bloody walked on!

Pure theatre!

A roar went up, the whole room stood: worth buying a ticket just to experience that. To get a standing ovation is one thing, but on your entrance, very special.

Shirley Bassey was doing a 3 week (sold out) season and although my involvement was over by the interval, I never left early, I never missed that entrance.

Imagine the confidence behind that decision,

"This is how we'll open the show, low key, no announcement."

That's when you KNOW you're a superstar!

ONWARDS, BUT NOT SO UPWARDS

Compering at Batley was a great experience. I was never exposed, doing my main spot at the best time before the audience became, shall I say, too 'boisterous'. I was meeting the big stars and it seemed like I was going places.

Then, in March 1973, something strange happened, I was closing the first half with a song, a terrific ballad by Jacque Brel, entitled 'If we only had Love'.

The song climbed dramatically, testing the upper range of my voice. I'd been feeling husky, my throat wasn't sore but felt strained; then on this occasion, as the music 'climbed', my voice wouldn't. The orchestration went higher, changing key, but I couldn't go with it.

Calamity: I'd gone from baritone to monotone!

Backstage, the bandleader, Tony Cervi, thought I'd been mucking about and had a go at me about 'ruining' the music, but when I convinced him I had a problem, he said: "laryngitis, mate. That's what that is".

I whispered through the rest of the show and the following morning booked to see a throat specialist. Complete rest was advised, no speaking for two weeks. I cancelled all my work. A fortnight later, there was no change, so I went in for an op to remove from my vocal chords, what were known as 'singer's nodules', which are small growths on the vocal chords caused by over use of the voice.

The operation was under full anaesthetic but when I came round the surgeon told me that, yes, although there were two small growths on the chords he hadn't removed them. To have done so, he said, would have resulted in scarring which might have affected my singing voice permanently.

"Only one thing for it," he said, "complete rest, no singing."

"For how long?"

"A month, maybe three."

"What?" I said (I didn't really, I couldn't speak).

My life was turned upside down, to perform and succeed at my level you needed a robust set of 'pipes'.

You couldn't 'walk' through a performance, you had to overcome background noise, plus the fact that smoking was permitted everywhere. A perfect scenario for ruining my voice permanently.

Then fate stepped in: just down the road from Glenfield Crescent in Chesterfield was the Aquarius nightclub, not as big as Batley but very popular and I heard that the compere, Eddie Buchanan, was moving on.

I figured I could get through working as their compere without singing, so I went to see the manager John Williamson and got the job. The money wasn't great but there were no travelling expenses plus, for some extra dosh, I could spend some time in the office booking the acts.

I'd really fallen on my feet. I'd found a compromise, still able to work AND protect my voice. I went in for a month and stayed for almost a year.

I was so lucky in many ways: I was earning, I was performing, plus I was learning about the booking procedures, talking to agents, etc. I was able to put a bill together, all the time working to a budget.

Even better, on stage I was being stretched, I had to be creative. The same people came week after week. I couldn't repeat any material so I locked the act away and winged it night after night. I'd interact with the audience, get them to interact with each other, swop their drinks, even their meals!

I'd find out where they were from, get them on stage, in fact I'd do anything,

It was inspiration born of desperation.

The experience served me well down the years, got me used to thinking on my feet and making something happen from nothing, something you can't buy, you have to earn it.

Plus, as a bonus, I was still able to protect my voice.

I've many stories to tell about my time at the Aquarius, but I'll tell you this one:

After a few months, I'd start taking the odd safe 'gig' where I knew my voice wouldn't be exposed. One such job came up in Leeds. I had an agreement with the Aquarius that I could put in a 'stand-in' compere for the night, so I rang Marti Caine.

Marti was a 'good turn' but, like the rest of us, hadn't had any real success at the time.

She was free on the night, I told her the money was ten quid, (going rate), and I left a cheque for her to collect from reception.

Two nights later I arrived back, Marti had been great, of course, she'd collected the envelope and all was well.

FAST FORWARD TWO YEARS: a lot had happened to Marti since she'd picked up that envelope.She'd entered 'New Faces', she'd won it, she'd starred in Las Vegas, she had her own TV series. In fact she'd become a big star!

Like everyone else who knew her, I was thrilled. She was so down to earth, a great lass and thoroughly deserved her 'overnight' (ha ha) success.

I hadn't seen her during those two years, so when I was in Swansea for a week's variety and saw that she was doing late-night cabaret at the Stoneleigh Club in Porthcawl, I drove over one night to catch up.

It was too late to see her before she went on so I sat at the back and when she came off, gave her a few minutes, went backstage and barged in.

"Surprise, surprise, Marti".

Oops, something not right as she looked at me daggers drawn.

"Clifton, sit down you bugger."

"What's up?"

"I'll tell you what's up."

She started rummaging in her handbag: "found it". She thrust a crumpled piece of paper under my nose.

"Do you know what that is?"

I studied it closely and recognised my writing and signature. It was my cheque!

"Come on, Clifton, what does it say?"

"Err, please pay Marti Caine ten pounds".

"Look at the bloody date"

Horror: I'd dated it a year earlier than I should have!

"Marti I'm so sorry. It was an accident, I promise. I'm really sorry".

She laughed like a loon: "I've been carrying that round in my handbag for two years, I knew I'd run into you sooner or later".

She accepted my mistake was genuine but she didn't let me off the hook totally, telling me: "I really needed that tenner back then".

The following night, I was back with a present for her that cost me more than a tenner.: a silver-plated mini champagne bucket plus tweezers for the ice.

It contained nothing more than a bottle of 'Coke', as I never saw her drink.

And that was our Marti, came up through the clubs, struggled like most of us and made it big, proper big.

For Marti to be taken from us so early was tragic. She was unique, a huge talent and more importantly a great lady.

I'm writing this after we've also lost Marti's best friend and 'stablemate', Sheffield's own Bobby Knutt, a terrific comic and actor.

So if you've met up, you two (and I like to think you have): "Sithee, see you sometime."

OFF TO JERSEY AGAIN

Early in 1974, and nine months into my Aquarius residency, who should pop in one night but my old Jersey producer Dick Ray, with an offer.

He was planning a Jersey summer season at a very prestigious venue, the Watersplash in St Brelades Bay. Would I be interested?

The money was much better than my compering salary and to massage my ego, I'd be joint top of the bill with Stuart Gillies, a fine singer who again, after a long time learning his craft, had won 'Opportunity Knocks' week after week after week.

I was at a crossroads, so comfortable living just round the corner from the Aquarius, but deep down I knew it was time to move on. I had many happy memories of my Jersey summer four years earlier but this was a much bigger challenge, one I was ready for. My voice was back, thanks to my lay-off, and I was having singing lessons to improve my technique. So, I said yes.

Madge was behind me as always, the kids were growing and we were planning to move to a bigger, detached house on the edge of town, so the money would help.

I'll never forget my Aquarius innings, nor will I ever forget my last night there. The band had organised an 'on-stage' party involving large quantities of crazy foam 'pie in the face' gags, so many that everyone wore industrial boiler suits for protection!

The day I had to head for Jersey came and there I was again, solo, heading south for the ferry, having spent my last night in Glenfield Crescent. We'd arranged to move house while I was in Jersey (as you do!).

This time I was following the nose of my Citroen DS23 Safari Estate, another one of my dream cars. It had hydro pneumatic suspension (or something similar) and swivelling headlights that looked round corners before you did. The kids loved this seven-seater, two of them facing sideways at the back. It was like driving a boat on a flat sea, so ahead of its time was it.

So now I'm back on the island that was to play such an important part in my career. The Watersplash was a great venue for all concerned. Stuart and I got on like a house on fire and again there was a great 'Jersey Company' feel about the place.

I started playing golf with the rest of the pros and it was an idyllic 70's summer season, one performance a night and the show going down a storm.

I only left the island once, this time with Dick Ray's blessing, on a day trip to Shepperton Film Studios. They were having a 'clear out' auction and there were some 'interesting' props going under the hammer. I'd never forgotten Les Dawson's advice: "Go and be a 'props' comic."

I got the first plane out, taxi from Heathrow, a couple of

successful bids at the auction and by late afternoon, I was back at Jersey Airport waiting for my baggage to appear on the carousel.

Let me define baggage: two huge rubber fish, one a 6ft-long shark, the other a 10ft-long 'grooper' (never mind the type, it was BIG).

The 'big un' had a series of motors inside to facilitate movement but they were on USA voltage and had to be removed, especially after they'd caught fire when I'd plugged them into a 13amp socket at my digs!

Don't ask about the house electrics, you can always get a 'sparkie' in Jersey if you're in the know. You CAN ask about the smell of burning rubber if you like, which took a while to clear, helped by lighting Joss sticks day and night. The house smelt like there was a hippy festival going on.

Stuart was already signed up to the Noel Gay agency, run by Richard Armitage, known in the business as R A, who's father, the original Noel Gay, had written so many hits back in the day.

Richard was a close friend of Billy Cotton Junior, who was now the head of BBC Light Entertainment and it was obvious I was mixing in the right circles.

It's all a question of 'right time, right place', isn't it?

People do get lucky, but best to be ready if Lady Luck ever comes to call!

I was renting Stuart's flat, adjoining his house and there was a connecting door. One afternoon it opened and there was Richard Armitage. And there I was, in me Y-fronts, ironing my shirts, face to face with R A, who was sporting a huge cigar,

"Hello, I'm Bernie."

"I know, saw your show last night...very good."

"Oh, thanks."

"Are you signed with another agency right now?"

"Err, no" (Where's this going?)

"Well, here's the deal, promise to sign with me and I'll promise to have Bill Cotton over to see you within three weeks. Have a think about it."

And he was gone, leaving behind the fragrance of a very expensive cigar.

To have someone of R A's stature asking you to sign was mind blowing. This was big league, as he had clients like songwriter Norman Newell, David Frost and many more.

I was shaking, not the best time to be ironing all (both) your stage shirts.

Is it really starting to happen? Hello, Lady Luck, is that you knocking?

She really was at the door, I did sign and three weeks later there was B C himself (no, I didn't ask him if his number plate was for sale and how much for cash).

A fortnight later Stewart Morris arrived, big-hitting senior BBC producer – Shirley Bassey Show and many more – something was afoot.

The show was a resounding success but here's autumn already, Weymouth beckoned and after months of pottering around the island I was soon putting miles on the Citroen clock.

I was at home for only a few days and got a call from Denmark St.

"Could you pop down for a meet, dear boy?"

I was on the train next day (when R A phones, you get up and go).

The headquarters of Noel Gay Music, in the centre of what was known as 'Tin Pan Alley', Denmark St itself, was an impressive building, three floors of agency partners handling every aspect of the business from circus performers to songwriters to music publishing to...northern 'turns'.

Richard Armitage was an amazing character. Highly regarded worldwide, he could pick up the phone to anyone, at any level, across the globe.

He sat back in his chair, cigar on the go of course, feet diagonally across the desk. Eyes twinkling behind horn-rimmed glasses.

"Good news, bad news, Bernard."

"Bad news first, from January, for three months, you'll be earning a quarter of what you usually earn."

"Good news, for those three months you'll be on television, BBC One, Saturday Night primetime, you're on the Lulu Show, dear boy."

"Happy?" he chortled.

I spluttered: "Absolutely".

"Off you go back 'OOP t'north, then".

(A lot of southern-based people could never quite 'get' the Northern way of clipping words together and usually overdid the vowel sounds, as happened in his case).

I floated through St Pancras on a cloud.

Me. On the telly, every Saturday night.

But not there yet.

I had already signed up with Thames Television to appear on 'Opportunity Knocks' the first weekend in November 1974. I'm not clear how this happened, it was obviously agreed before the Lulu deal came up.

Of the two horses the Opps Knocks steed was the one I'd rather not get on but I had to.

To make matters worse...the whole Watersplash Show with guests was going north that week. (How far north? Glasgow, is that far enough?)

So here's my schedule for that period:

Sunday: drive to Glasgow

Mon/Tues/Wed/Thurs: Pavilion Theatre, two shows per night.

Friday: up at dawn, drive Citroen to Glasgow airport, shuttle to Heathrow, taxi to Teddington, rehearse 'Opps Knocks', taxi to Heathrow, shuttle to Glasgow, drive to theatre, two shows then bed.

(If you're wondering why I've mentioned the Citroen, read on).

Saturday: up at dawn, drive Citroen to airport, shuttle to Heathrow, rehearse/record 'Opps Knocks', taxi to Heathrow, shuttle to Glasgow, drive to theatre, two shows, pack props into Citroen, drive overnight to Chesterfield (5 hours).

Sunday morning: drive to Lakeside Club, Camberley, Surrey (5 hours), arrive late afternoon for band call then 45-minute cabaret spot at 11 pm, drive to digs and bed.

That itinerary makes me think that someone trying to kill me.

There's worse: I've omitted a teeny, weeny detail.

On the Friday early morning commute to Glasgow Airport, it was obvious that something was wrong with the car. On the Friday evening return trip, it became clear it was the exhaust. So on Saturday, during my leisure time (ha!), I ordered a new exhaust from the Chesterfield dealer to be delivered to my home on Saturday afternoon.

My Saturday night/Sunday morning journey south, with the exhaust hanging off, was erm…interesting.

I awoke from a fevered sleep on Sunday morning to the noise of a mechanic on my drive doing the work. Got up, had breakfast and drove to Camberley in the heavy Sunday traffic, hence another five hours.

I've not finished yet: Word had filtered back to Richard that during my 'Opps Knocks' appearance I didn't appear to be at my best, (now why would that be?) and wouldn't do my career prospects any good.

In those days, there were very few video recorders. If you didn't see a TV Show live, it was gone. So R A hatched a plan, he arranged to take the relevant 'Lulu' producers to see me perform at the Lakeside on the following Monday, the same evening that my 'Opps Knocks' appearance was being transmitted. As they'd be en route, there'd be no chance they would see me on on screen.

The show went out at 6.45, so he collected them well before then, driving them to Camberley ensuring they would be 'in transit' at the time and, as he said later, "hoping we wouldn't stop at the lights in Camberley High Street outside Currys window while the show was on".

Skullduggery and messy to boot, but it illustrates the madness that goes on behind the scenes.

SATURDAY NIGHT ON THE TELLY

The Lulu series duly arrived but I have to admit the exposure wasn't great for me, it was okay, but I didn't deliver for the cameras the way I did for an audience when I worked live.

One of the guests on the series was Tessie O'Shea. I'd worked with Tessie a couple of years earlier in Blackpool and we were good friends.

She said: "Bernie, my love, there's something missing when you're on camera. I don't know what it is but you're not the same, you gotta find out what it is and fix it."

I don't know if I ever did.

There were many theories of how to fix this.

One was to look into the lens as if it was a window into someone's front room, with just three people watching you. But to me at the time, those big cameras felt like obstacles between me and the audience.

I'm sorry that the series didn't turn out to be the launch pad it should have been, but I was still getting chances.

Work was still pouring in. I'd been 'elevated' if that's the right word, up to the cabaret circuit and my club experience stood me in good stead. I had a strong act, very visual with the props and very different from the 'patter comics' I was working alongside plus, as a bonus, my voice was in good shape which meant, after all the nonsense, my act had a big finish.

CHAPTER 10
ALONG CAME THE DUCK

My list of props was growing and whenever I met up with Les Dawson, I always thanked him for his advice.

I had the biscuit tins, the fish, the lion and, in Jersey, I'd developed an idea that involved wearing a cape. I was a fan of the Marx Brothers and saw Harpo wearing a big overcoat with various sound effects emanating from the folds as he pressed them.

The Strawberry Farm in Jersey had a Halloween night and the daughter had made a stuffed black cat for the witch. They gave me the cat and I used to pin it on my shoulder to 'interrupt' Stuart at the end of our show.

I gave the cat to the genius that is Peter Pullon, to see if he could improve it. Peter made props large and small for everyone including Rod Hull's Emu; and for Keith Harris, he designed Cuddles and Orville. He had a workshop in Coventry and I was a frequent visitor, fascinated to see these animals coming alive in his hands.

The cape arrived via the 'Desert Song' musical score,

featuring the Red Shadow, so all I needed was some mischief to put under the cape.

I was backstage at a club in Wales and, noticing some large gas cylinders stood against the wall, asked the stage manager what they were for.

"We use it for the beer, let me show you."

He opened the nozzle and a huge jet of white vapour shot out.

I had a 'Eureka' moment: I could get one of those under my cape.

Then a 'Desert Song' parody came to mind...

"Lonely as a desert breeze, get that breeze between your knees".

What's that rustling sound? That'll be Sigmund Romberg turning in his grave.

The routine was coming together, it had...cat on shoulder, for no real reason; full-length red cape; concealed gas cylinder; plus lyrics to die for.

First time I tried it out (at Batley Variety Club), the cylinder I'd borrowed was far too big and heavy and the jet of gas too powerful to control.

I sang "Lonely as a Desert Breeze", opened the nozzle and was blown flat on my back with a cloud of vapour roaring from under my red cloak, staining it white in the process: not a pretty sight!

It's clear my act it needed work that's all. What was also clear was the thirst I had for visual comedy.

Around this time someone told me about someone they'd seen in street carnival apparently 'riding' a chicken. I spoke to Peter and he knew exactly what I meant.

He came up with a series of sketches and went to work.

He warned me the prototype would be crude but it would be somewhere to start, a kind of template.

I busied myself with my Red Shadow routine while gigging around the country and a few weeks later Peter rang me, said he'd come up with something and said: "come and have a go".

I went to see him and there it was. A large yellow fluffy object on the floor of his workshop. Not too impressive I thought, as Peter suggested I 'jumped on'.

It felt strange but I thought I'd test it by going outside on the street. Immediately there was a reaction in the rush-hour traffic as I weaved in and out of the cars. The Job Centre was opposite, so I ran in and caused a fair amount of chaos as I enquired about vacancies for Ostrich Jockeys.

The 'test' completed, we both agreed it was another 'work in progress' project and I suppose that was the secret. Over the next few years, we invested a lot in 'breeding' a realistic beast. Along the way there were many failures. I remember using it on Crackerjack and it barely registered. In fact, I saw the episode recently on DVD and it was a mess.

Eventually, thanks to Peter's skills and determination, we felt we had something. During the 'breeding', our research reinforced the saying that there's 'nothing new in comedy'. Around 1914, a music hall owner and entrepreneur from Nottingham had a similar beast made from papier mache, he called it his 'Daddio' and wrote a song to go along with the prop. Sadly, he came to a sticky end, apparently 'falling off' it while drunk and injuring himself and never worked again.

The adage 'nothing new' cropped up again around that time. It was 1978, I was doing a week at Cesars Palace Night Club in Luton and after the show, chatted to the trombonist, telling him how I loved the trombone. I liked to hear it played but was fascinated by the comedy potential of the instrument. During the conversation I thought, 'wouldn't it be brilliant if, while you were playing the trombone, you could make your trouser legs go up and down'.

This time I went to another prop genius with my idea. Bill King was a legend when it came to props. Nothing was impossible for him.

Here's an example: years ago, I was driving to London to do the Russell Harty late-night TV chat show. As I joined the M1 at Junction 29, I heard news of the Brinksmatt gold bullion robbery at Heathrow. I pulled in at Leicester Forest services, phoned Bill from a payphone and asked him if he'd got any gold bars (not real ones),

"How many do you want?" was his off-hand reply.

"Enough to fill a brief case."

"When do you want em?"

"Tonight, at the Greenwich Theatre."

And there they were, in a brief case, at the stage door when I arrived.

The gag went like this: as Russell was interviewing Zsa Zsa Gabor, I entered, on the ostrich, much to the consternation of the lovely Zsa Zsa (who, by the way, in spite of being a mature lady, resembled a beautiful porcelain doll).

"Ooh darlink, don't come near me with that theenk. Eet is scarink mee to death".

So I kept my distance and shouted to the host.

"Sorry I'm late, Russell, had some trouble at Heathrow" as I released the catch on the brief case and the gold bars fell out. Call me Mr Topical!

So that was Bill's pedigree, he could do ANYTHING. He did all the Crackerjack special effects and if Morecambe and Wise did anything visual, it would be down to Sir Bill, his fingerprints would be all over it.

His base in West London was an Aladdin's Cave, dripping from floor to ceiling with weird and wonderful props.

He went to work for me and created a wonderfully 'rigged' costume. As the trombone slide went out, the trouser legs went up, either together or independently, and vice versa. As a finale (cos with sophisticated stuff like this folks, you need a way to get off), I pulled a pin and the trousers ended up around my ankles. And they said satire was dead!

During my 1979 summer, I drove to Poole on Sunday for a BBC 'Summertime Special'. I rehearsed the trombone/trouser gag in the afternoon and when I'd finished, the producer Michael Hurll came up to me and said: "Great stuff, Bernie, that trombone routine I haven't seen since Lupino Lane did it at the Palladium in 1948".

I was flabbergasted. I really thought it was my idea but, in a way, flattered that I was on the same wavelength of one of the all-time greats.

I recently lent the outfit to my mate, the talented Richard Gauntlett (proppy kind of guy), so he could make a copy. He's a lot younger than I am and it's right that stuff should be handed on.

IF YOU CAN'T DRIVE IT, FLY IT

My obsession with aviation will emerge later on. Perhaps it was kindled by those few flights I had in the RAF and, during the Seventies, flying became necessary because of my workload.

During my 1977 summer season in Lowestoft, at the

Sparrows Nest Theatre, one of the attractions of a garden fete I was opening was a low-level flypast in Chipmunk I think by a local man, former jet pilot Keith Nunn. We became great friends and I took him up on his offers of a flight whenever I could.

Keith and his fellow pilots came to my aid on a very sad occasion that year. My older brother John tragically died from a cancer-related illness in September. We were all devastated for him to be taken, aged just 43, but even worse for me, based in Suffolk for the summer and working Monday to Saturday, there was no way I could get to the funeral in St Helens.

Keith was brilliant, he organised a pilot and a plane so I was able to be with my folks at this awful time and back in Lowestoft for that evening's performance.

A bleak example of 'the show must go on' but I'd never have got through it without the help of Keith and his team.

I was offered a one nighter in Perranporth, Cornwall which I accepted because it was during a two-night break I had from a short season at the the Theatre Royal in...erm, NORWICH!

Keith arranged the plane and with all my props in the back, took off on a beautiful sunny morning. We had a low-level clearance over central London, which gave me a fantastic view of the capital. The flight was uneventful and we landed at Perranporth Airport a few hours later. I unloaded my props by the side of the runway, which was being used by the local Gliding Club. I watched the Norfolk Aviators take off and wandered over to the control tower to see about getting a cab to the venue, Perran Sands Holiday Camp, just a few miles away.

My arrival had attracted some interest amongst the occupants of the clubhouse, all members of the local gliding fraternity. Perhaps it wasn't my arrival that raised eyebrows but more likely the fact that by the side of their runway lay an apparently dead ostrich, a cat, a CO2 cylinder, a red cloak, a pair of biscuit tins with the Legend, 'Clifton's Crackers' emblazoned on the sides, a microphone stand and a 12ft-long rubber fish.

Because of the limited storage space in the aeroplane, none of these objects were 'boxed' and lay there for all to see.

There wasn't a cab available but one of the members offered his car. We crammed the props inside and with the fish's tail waving from the rear window, left the scene.

The show went well and the following morning, helped by my Good Samaritan of the previous day, I was back with said accessories laid out on the grass awaiting the arrival of my air taxi for the return trip.

It proved to be a long wait, as by mid afternoon was no sign of the plane. The phone calls became more frantic as the day wore on. Eventually I was told that because of bad weather over Dartmoor, he'd been forced to turn back to Norfolk.

There was only one option, a train trip, and the Good Samaritan who had helped me earlier earn many more Brownie points as we filled his car with props again and tore off to Truro Railway Station in a desperate attempt to catch the Penzance Express, the last train to Paddington.

As we screeched to a halt by the entrance, the train had just arrived, so no time to buy a ticket. Everyone swooped to help, both station staff and amused onlookers.

What a bizarre sight: A posse (of hitherto strangers) charging across the footbridge, with me in the lead holding a sleeping ostrich while bellowing "STOP THAT TRAIN".

And we made it. I waved goodbye to my saviours,

unable to thank my Good Samaritan properly (and I'm afraid I never did).

Even more kindness was waiting at Paddington. Keith had driven over to take me and my props back to Norwich, a six-hour round trip for him.

Unbelievable – what a star! It wasn't his fault the weather had turned nasty and yet he'd dropped everything to help.

As for my unknown Cornwall 'taxi man', wherever you are I'm very still grateful!

Some people are just terrific!

However on another occasion the saying, 'Time to spare? Go by Air', came back to bite me again…

This time, Keith was to fly me from Clacton, where I was working, over to the Isle of Wight for yet another one nighter. The weather closed in and I had to leap in my car for a long, arduous return drive. (Only a couple of inches on the map!).

After the gig, I was too late to catch the midnight ferry so I slept in the car and got the first one out. So, virtually no sleep and after another four-hour drive, I turned up at my digs in Norwich, crashing into bed, being woken after just a few hours as I had an afternoon show to appear in.

In spite of these adventures my obsession with flying had begun in earnest.

CHAPTER 11
SOME GREAT NEWS!

JUST before I started a Weston-super-Mare season, I'd done a one-nighter at Blazers Club in downtown Windsor. I didn't realise until I got there that it was some kind of showbiz charity evening. I was not 'fazed', however, as I had an act that worked. Blazers was a great space to perform and I was down to do no more than 15/20 minutes.

I was on with Patti Boulay and Peter Gordeno and his dancers. My turn came and I had a REALLY fine time, as I crammed the ostrich and the Red Shadow into the time allowed and it all went down a storm.

Little did I know...

I was in my Weston digs a little while later – it was a bungalow in a village called Hutton nearby – when my landlady who lived next door shouted over the wall in her lovely West Country accent: "Bernie...phone".

There wasn't a phone in the bungalow, mobiles hadn't been invented so she kindly let me have the use of hers. I went round, picked up the phone and it was the unmistakable rich baritone of R A himself that greeted me.

"Ah, dear boy, I've just had a call from Louis Benjamin, do you know the name?"

Of course, L B was a big name in London and beyond.

"He saw you the other night at Blazers, said you came on with a parrot on your shoulder." (So Louis Benjamin, one of the most powerful men in show business, can't tell the difference between a parrot and a bloody cat!).

"Anyway, he's putting a little show together in November and he definitely wants you to be part of it: you AND the parrot."

He was chortling now, the way he did when he told me I'd got the Lulu show.

"So that's good news, isn't it?".

"Great."

"Even more good news, dear boy," (the chortle was no longer suppressed and had gone up an octave") "the little show in question is the Royal Variety Show in front of the Queen and you're on it, yes, you're definitely on it".

Oh, my Auntie Norah: GOOSE BUMPS! (Never mind back then, I've got them even now as I relive the call).

The Royal Variety Show – in front of the Queen! Me! (And me parrot, who does cat impressions).

I was bursting to tell the world, but I couldn't. It had to be a secret for a while and, anyway, I couldn't have told anyone from next door's phone.

First chance I got I was down to the village with me bag of coins, I swore Madge to secrecy and gave her the news. We shared a few tears during that call, I can tell you. More than twenty years of working in all those pubs and clubs, living in a caravan with three kids and now this, the Royal Variety Show.

It was every performer's dream and mine was coming true. That singer who gave up the title 'world's worst plumber' would be meeting the Queen.

I also broke the news to Len Lowe, who was producing and appearing in our summer show. A former double act with his brother Don, he was one of those people who everyone respected. Much older than I was, but still very smart and dapper (great word, dapper).

A lovely guy and the world's greatest' straight man', I'd describe him as 'old school' and, believe me, that's a compliment. He'd worked alongside some of our greatest comics, knew every gag in the book and a few more besides.

I'd have the honour of working with him over the years to come in some great two- and three-handed sketches. There was no one better than Uncle Len, because he knew the value of the 'straight man'.

I've done sketches, in and out of panto, with other comics and it depends on the role play. Can a comic who's spent a lifetime looking for laughs swap identity for the sake of the sketch? Not everyone can and not everyone wants to.

The trombone routine I mentioned earlier never worked better than when I did it with Len. He'd go on stage carrying a trumpet, giving the impression he was about to play it and talking with great authority on the music you were about to hear (but never played).

I would appear as 'helper' to set the mike and music stands, placing the music in position but generally causing chaos which continued until I brought on my trusty 'trumpet'.

"That's not a trumpet."

"Got it free with a crumpet, hope I don't bump it."

"Be quiet."

Mumbles: "If you don't like, it you can lump it."

(And so on, till the 'Trouser' gag ending). Can't beat ending on a 'visual'!

R A was 'on it' when it came to the Royal Variety Show (henceforth known as the RVS). His influence became apparent by the phone call I got one day,

"Hi, is that Bernie, Richard Armitage gave me your number, he thinks I might be able to help you write some material for this little concert you're doing in November."

"Oh right, sorry, I didn't catch your name."

"Neil Shand." (Neil bloody Shand, only one of the country's top comedy writers).

During the next few weeks, my life went into overdrive: meetings with Neil Shand to work on the script; music to arrange and plenty of conversations with Bill King.

Bill once told me how he had employed his skills during World War Two. He was involved in the resistance movement in German-occupied Europe. Bill and his colleagues would take a stuffed (or recently dead) rat and pack it with high explosives. The resistance fighters, employed in German-run factories, would smuggle in the rodent and leave it near the factory furnace before leaving the area.

A patrolling soldier, seeing the corpse, would pick it up and (what else would he do?) toss it into the flames, with obvious consequences.

That was a far cry from the job I was giving him, as I was asking for a second ostrich. An ostrich with a moving head and neck, but that could move independently from me.

Bill was just the man to create this extra 'beast' or, as it became known, the 'empty ostrich'. With his customary deadpan "no problem", he went to work.

Realising this was a once-in-a-lifetime opportunity, I set about the project as one might plan a military operation. No stone was left unturned. Originally, R A felt that I was packing too much into the eight-minute spot, but I held my ground as the pieces fell into place and the date became ever closer.

My' team', at this time, consisted of Bill King, 'empty ostrich' builder; Geoff Thacker, empty ostrich 'operator', (he was then a dancer who would go on to be a TV director at the highest level, including at least one Royal Command Performance); Lesley Wootton, choreographer, (I'd worked with her in Jersey and she was invaluable in staging the whole thing); Paul Mathews, musical director, (my regular 'on the road' pianist); Nigel de Lory, road manager, (a real 'go to' man and possessor of a huge handlebar moustache, he was such a calming influence and kept me sane. Great character, I owe him a lot!).

WHAT A TEAM!

I was surrounded by talent, people at the top of their game and even better, really nice people and good friends. Plus, I had all my family (including kids) who came on board with lots of 'ostrich feet combing' and many wardrobe 'tweaks'.

Last but not least, I couldn't have coped without John and Sue Adams. John was a senior production manager at the BBC and heavily involved in 'Crackerjack'. After a couple of weeks into the series, he asked me where I disappeared to as soon as rehearsals finished for the day. When I told him, St Pancras, for my daily commute to Chesterfield, he was aghast: "You must be mad, you're killing yourself. Look, I've got a big house in Teddington, why not come and stay with me?".

Well, to be honest, the commute was killing me, so I took him up on his offer. That was in 1976 and as I never tire of telling everyone, he never managed to get rid of me.

We are best friends to this day, his boy Christopher is my godson and John still refers to his back bedroom in Cambridge Road as 'your room'.

I can't overstate the role all these special people have played in my life.

I was still a northern boy at heart, out of my comfort zone in London and the fact that I still felt the need to travel home every night speaks for itself. But thanks to John's generosity, I was able to relax and enjoy my time in the capital. Good eggs, John and Sue.

MEETING THE QUEEN - AND THE 'KING OF SIAM'

The great day came and, as Nigel helped me unload the props at the stage door of the Theatre Royal, Drury Lane, I felt excited and slightly apprehensive. Everyone had worked so hard and we'd done as much as possible. I was ready, ready to meet Royalty, and even the King…of Siam?

Yul Brynner was on the show. He was doing a medley of songs from the 'King and I'.

I'd just finished my rehearsal and, astride the ostrich, careered round a corner backstage to come face to face with the King of Siam. There he was in his full royal costume, looking at a man…sitting on an ostrich!

He took a pace backwards, startled. Then he drew himself up to his full 'height' (not that tall, was our Yul), put his hands on his hips and, gazing at me in disbelief, gave a sort of strangled "HARRUMPH".

I didn't know whether to say "Hello, your Majesty" or, perhaps, "Ey Up, Yul", but I did neither, I just gave him a quick curtsey and made my exit.

Backstage, it was lunacy: I was sharing a dressing room with a lot of big names, including Jim Davidson and Noel Edmonds. As for the stars performing that night, I was the only one I'd never heard of! Here's a few: Bill Haley and his Comets, James Mason, Carol Channing, Yul Brynner, Red Buttons, Janet Brown, Marti Caine and Les Dawson.

Because of the cramped conditions backstage, most of the performers sat in the theatre stalls awaiting their turn to rehearse. Can you imagine how I felt when it was my turn, seeing these faces watching me?

It would have been so easy to have become submerged by this galaxy of talent but, thanks to my team, I was so well prepared that the rehearsal went well.

As showtime loomed, the tension was palpable. I had some good friends backstage, amongst them Len Lowe, my Weston-super-Mare producer who, along with fellow Water Rats, was involved with the charity benefiting from the evening.

He came round and whispered: "The Queen's here, she's in the building".

Even now, writing this, I can feel my heart skipping a beat.

Then I was on, this was it! Waiting in the wings, I was watching Janet Brown and Carol Channing doing a 'Margaret Thatcher' routine which was going really well and, I thought: "You're as ready as you'll ever be, go out and enjoy it". And I did!

I was out there, fit as a butcher's dog, performing at 100 miles an hour, and I got an audience reaction beyond my wildest dreams. Between the orchestra and the front row was a semi-circular 'catwalk'. The ostrich chose to take this route, at full gallop, with devastating effect. It was a riot, everything worked, and eight minutes later, I came off to a huge ovation.

Len Lowe was waiting for me: "Did you see the Queen, she was in tears, crying with laughter, she'd got the hankie out".

I hadn't seen the Queen, as we were ordered not to look (I was too scared, anyway).

Richard Armitage came backstage: "You did it, you did it!"

I was in a dream, walking on air.

Then it was time for the Royal line-up to meet her Majesty. It was a blur, she gave me such a dazzling smile, remarking on how funny I'd been and how fit I must be. I explained that I'd trained seriously for the event.

I'll never forget that smile and remember, up close, how beautiful she was.

I have a large framed photograph which captured the moment perfectly.

At the reception a tall, distinguished man shook my hand and congratulated me, telling me how I had taken the show 'by storm' and that first thing the following morning, he would be phoning my agent to offer me my own TV series.

Was this a joke?

I had no idea who he was and didn't really take in what he said. I was told he was none other than Jon Scoffield, the show's producer. Jon was head of light entertainment for ATV, the ITV company who were televising the event.

I caught up with Madge who, along with John and Sue, were having a fine time as the theatre emptied, sitting in the Royal Box giving the royal wave to passing stagehands.

Then it was back to Teddington, thanking Nigel for recovering my car from the police pound where it had been removed to. It had been parked opposite the stage door and was considered to be a 'security risk' (Nigel took all this in his stride, Top Man, our 'Nige').

Up at dawn, too pumped up to sleep, so I went out to buy all the papers. In those days, the show was 'leaked' immediately and my reviews were very favourable. It was transmitted the following weekend, and I watched it on a small black-and-white portable TV I had backstage at a theatre I was working in, which tells you I was back in the groove.

CHAPTER 12
INTO THE EIGHTIES

MY RVS appearance was well received and Jon Scoffield was true to his word. Following various meetings, I was booked to do my own TV Special in May, 1980, followed by a series from the Theatre Royal, Nottingham, entitled 'Summer Royal'.

The 'Special' was my big chance. A team was assembled. I got together with the producer Royston Mayoh; two up-and-coming writers, Andrew Marshall and David Renwick (who were to go on to become amazingly successful); and none other than Len Lowe, and we came up with a format.

Because I had this penchant for 'props', we would build a stage full of trapdoors. I would bang my foot, a trapdoor would open and a 'prop' would emerge.

The show title: 'Bernie Clifton Onstage'.

We were bouncing ideas off each other and I was pretty excited...

However, (with me, there's always been an 'however'!), prior to the RVS, I'd signed a contract for a month-long tour of Australia, specifically the clubs in Sydney. My previous trips had been very successful and I always looked forward to my annual 'Down Under' visits.

But not this time, as the Aussie trip clashed with the run-up to my TV Special. At this point, here comes a series of the most useless phrase known to man…' should have'.

I 'should have' got out of that Aussie contract and I 'should have' said: "I'm not going. Buy me out, whatever it costs, I'm not going".

I still don't know why I didn't take that course of action. I made a mistake. I lacked the hard-nosed business acumen to make the right decision.

I've been around a few big stars over the years. They have two things in common: talent, of course, but more than that, they all had a sense of business, an awareness of what was right for them.

But me, I went to Sydney, did a few clubs and, before Skype, Facetime, et al, sat by the pool all day, wondering what was happening to my career.

The tour over, I flew back, went directly from Heathrow to Elstree Studios and, jet-lagged after a 24-hour flight, began my rehearsals for 'Onstage'.

We also did some filming at Towcester Racecourse and, two weeks later, we recorded the show in front of a studio audience. The idea of the stage dotted with trapdoors worked well. It was alright on the night and the show got reasonable reviews when it was shown but, like the Lulu series five years earlier, I have to admit it was another 'near miss' for me.

So although I'd moved up considerably from being a club 'turn', I still hadn't 'nailed' a proper TV career.

I was, however, busier than ever, touring clubs and

theatres and then the 'Summer Royal' series in Nottingham.

I had our 'Crackerjack' writer Tony Hare on board, along with my brother Michael, plus another 'B.C', the comedy genius, Barry Cryer. They all contributed material for my spots and to avoid any confusion as to who had written what, Barry suggested he would type his stuff in capital letters only, to earn the title of 'Barry Big Print'.

The 'Summer Royal' series had a resident Company of talented Singers and Dancers, including Sue Pollard, who was to go on to star as Peggy the Chalet Maid in 'Hi de Hi' (and, more recently, my Las Vegas housemate).

We rehearsed in London for three days, then drove up to Nottingham for three nights of 'live' variety, giving me the chance to run the material destined for the Sunday TV show.

I was having trouble sleeping at the time, and when Bob Monkhouse came in to headline our Sunday show, I mentioned the problem. The hotel had no aircon and I was 'frying' at night (opening the windows wasn't an option because of traffic noise).

Bob left after the show but, two days later, I got a small parcel he'd posted. It contained an eye mask, earplugs and a short note brilliantly illustrated by a cartoon he'd drawn.

Imagine: as if he wasn't busy enough, he'd gone home and immediately sat down and put the 'pack' together for me!

I enjoyed my time in Nottingham but, then again, I always did. For twenty years, from the street corner pubs to the big Miners Social Clubs, I'd always found its 'natives' very friendly. To turn up and be greeted, "Ey up, me duck", was always a good sign.

The Matcham-designed Theatre Royal is a beautiful

building, a brilliant space to perform in and I've many happy memories of my times there, including the 'Jimmy Tarbuck Jape' I opened this book with.

L.A.C (LIFE AFTER 'CRACKERJACK')

After four years, my 'Crackerjack' days were over. It was like being in a repertory company, but on television. A change of programme every week, make do and mend, thinking on your feet. We performed it 'as live', our various directors, from Bill Wilson to Alan J Bell, telling us: "you'd better get it right because if you make a mistake, the whole country will see it on Friday" (at 5-to-5 of course).

The best bit for me was our outdoor filming days, which were done in the style of the 'Keystone Cops' silent movies.

Peter Glaze, Jan Hunt, Ed Stewart and I would turn up at the crack of dawn at some out-of-the-way location. It could be a Zoo, a derelict gasworks, a boatyard, whatever the script demanded. I say script, but much of it was made up as we went along. Then director Alan Bell (amongst his many future credits, 'Last of the Summer Wine'), might ring up the crew on the morning of the shoot and say: "Bring a ladder and I need some straw hats and buckets, plenty of buckets" (or whatever was in his head).

He had us risking life and limb, hanging from roofs, swallowing gallons of foam, standing knee-deep in freezing water, but you name it and we did it. He even had Peter Glaze, during a circus sketch, stand in a lion's cage, face to face with the King of the Jungle, who cocked his head and looked at Peter with a curious look that said, "lunch?". I saw the DVD recently and there was no camera trickery; it was for real.

I did try to reassure Peter prior to the event: "Don't worry, Peter, if the lion should attack, there's a man standing by with a high-powered rifle",

"Rifle?", a grey-faced Peter asked,

"Yes, to save any unnecessary pain, he'll shoot you".

Happy days!

But it was time to move on. The Eighties had dawned and my life had changed. One side effect of my newfound fame was my loss of anonymity.

We lived on a main road and, quite often late on Saturday nights, the youth of the town took to driving up and down, leaning out of their cars, shouting "Crackerjack".

Hilarious: no, not really.

So weekends found us looking for a move to the country. The places we were looking at were usually rundown smallholdings. One property springs to mind and not just because of its name. Pudding Pie Farm lay to the west of Chesterfield and it ticked a few of my boxes, but Madge and the kids were not impressed,

"We're not living out here, there's no buses for a start."

Of course, they were right, but they tolerated my yearning to live in the country.

So on a bright December Sunday afternoon, we were gazing in silence at this derelict barn of a building when the peace was broken by the sound of a distant lawnmower. We couldn't see it, but it was getting louder and louder and then…a man appeared, sitting on the 'lawnmower' which was attached to a pair of wings, casually waving as he flew overhead.

"WHAT IS THAT?" I shouted, followed by, "I WANT ONE."

I was stunned by what I'd just seen. It was not a flying

lawnmower, of course. It was my first sighting of a new type of flying machine, and I was hooked.

I spent the next week tracking down the pilot, Eric Barfoot, who was a local builder and had got into flying by hang gliding in the Peak District.

But he'd grown tired of lugging it up hills, assembling it, then relying on the wind to go flying. So by bolting a two-stroke engine under the wing, a propellor out the back, and lying face down underneath the contraption, they would risk life and limb to go flying.

The powered hang glider was soon followed by the Microlight, which is what I'd seen. The pilot was seated on his 3-wheel' lawnmower', which hung under the wing. With the engine over his head, propellor buzzing away behind him, he could take off from any small, flat field.

I was fascinated by all this. The thought of buzzing around at 500 feet was really up my street, and a few months later, I found myself at Langar Airfield, near Nottingham, aiming to become a pilot. The training was run by an American couple, Barry and his wife, Sue. Following a short talk, we trooped out to see our' winged chariot'.

The 'Eagle' Microlight had a tricycle undercarriage that, in flight, hung under a large hang glider-type wing. Also hung under the wing was the pilot, who sat in a sort of cradle that swung to and fro. The pilot gripped handlebars with a motorbike-type throttle. Pretty basic really, and push the seat back to go up and vice versa to come down.

My first question was, "where does the instructor sit?"

I found Barry's drawled reply disconcerting: "It's a single-seater; you go up on your own".

He explained that, to start with, I'd be towed up and

down the runway to get used to the controls but my first journey into the wide blue yonder would be solo.

Following this bombshell, and perhaps coincidentally, by the second day the class of twelve aspiring aviators had shrunk by half! The missing six had probably realised they had better things to do with the rest of their lives and, bowing out at that stage, might ensure they had a 'rest of a life' to look forward to.

The rest of us were surprised to hear Barry say that "today was 'going solo' day". Obviously, I joined the rush to the back of the queue. One by one, the trainees were strapped in, patted on the head and told to go for it. Amazingly, they limped into the air, did a circuit, and returned to earth in various ways that could vaguely be described as 'landings'.

Number four, named Spike, who'd told me he was a parachutist, had, when it was his turn, what I'd better describe as a 'downstairs emergency' and took off (sorry, wrong phrase) on foot, at speed, heading for some distant bushes.

I was sixth and last, when the fifth trainee, a large man with a West Country accent (that's not really important) was strapped in, but as he was being patted on the head he told Barry: "I'm alright, but I've decided to do it tomorrow".

"Excuse me," drawled Barry.

"Yes, I'll be doing it tomorrow."

"Don't worry, you'll be fine."

"Oh, I am fine really, but I'm doing it tomorrow".

Barry was very cool and did his best to calm the guy down but, after ten minutes, gave up and helped him out of the saddle.

Which meant it was my turn. I looked over my

shoulder, no movement in the bushes (I'm sure the opposite was true!). I had no option but to climb in and following the head pat, went for it.

The most vivid memories of that 10 minutes in my life? Nerve jangling, buttock-clenching eye-watering TERROR!

I could feel the vomit rising in my throat as I swung about, the twin Chrysler two-stroke roaring over my head. My panic had put my muscles into spasm as I'd gone for full throttle, and I was unable to level off.

There I was, about to die, nose up at 45 degrees, what a way to go! I remember thinking, please God, if you'll let me off this once, I'll never do anything like this again.

I looked down for the first time and I saw a few clouds, a scenario that hadn't been covered in training (you'd see clouds, of course, but not from above).

Through the gaps in the clouds, I saw some cows and wished I could swap places (I'd rather be down there chewing cud than up here tasting vomit).

Honestly, I was on the point of being sick from sheer fright but calmed down when I realised there was only one person who could get me down in one piece…ME!

I managed to gain some degree of control, complete a sort of circuit, descend slowly and somehow land the thing, emerging physically, if not emotionally, intact.

As soon as I was down, though, I wanted to go up again but couldn't because of the weather closing in.

As many a pilot will tell you, flying is very addictive. Once you've been up there on your own, you're bitten by the bug and I was well and truly hooked.

Sadly, for various reasons, subsequent visits to the airfield didn't yield another flight. I was about to start a summer season in Great Yarmouth, so I did a deal with the flying school and left for the seaside with a second-hand Eagle on my roof rack.

I persuaded a friendly farmer to let me fly from his land and couldn't wait to get airborne again. Then, I thought, why not get some publicity, so I rang the Daily Mirror and they said they'd send someone.

A few days later, having assembled the Eagle myself, I proudly wheeled it out to show Mike Maloney, the photographer, who seemed very impressed. I'd also glued some letters to the wings and the Eagle had now become the 'Flying Ostrich'.

Mike was less impressed when I explained I wasn't a proper pilot yet but he agreed to snap me, on the 'Ostrich', in front of the aeroplane.

He then asked: "Can you get in the plane on the ostrich?"

A few minutes later, I was onboard, still astride the ostrich.

"Can you taxi up and down the runway a bit?"

Even though it was very uncomfortable, I managed to trundle up and down the field as he'd suggested, but he still wasn't happy,

"What I need is daylight between the wheels and the ground".

"Sorry Mike, but I'm not really a pilot. I don't know how to fly the thing, I've only been up once, which was a bit scary, and at the time I wasn't sitting on an ostrich".

Mr Maloney wouldn't give in: "I need to see daylight under the wheels, otherwise I haven't got a picture".

So back and forth I went, managing to 'hop' a few feet from Mother Earth.

"Higher, higher," he shouted.

Sod it, he's not going to give in, so I went for it. A few

seconds later, I roared down the field and soared into the air. There I was, at 500 feet, in an aeroplane I couldn't fly, sitting on an ostrich thinking, 'I'm going to die for the Daily Mirror'.

As terrified as I was, I managed some kind of landing without breaking anything.

A few days later, the article appeared in the Daily Mirror. The only photograph used was about two inches square and, if you studied it through a magnifying glass, you might have just been able to make out the shape of a large bird and, on its back, a man with a very pale face.

Looking back, I realise I was very stupid and very lucky. The Eagle was a very forgiving, slow aeroplane but that day I'd broken all the rules and all for the sake of a tiny picture in a national newspaper. Never again.

Although I often flew the plane that summer, it was never on an ostrich and never for a publicity stunt.

However, the nearest I got to shake hands with the Grim Reaper happened that summer, not in the air but on the A12 coming out of Great Yarmouth. I was following an articulated lorry carrying a stack of huge steel plates. As he turned sharp left onto the road bridge, I was able to overtake,

As I did so, for some reason, he slammed on his brakes, causing the lorry to jackknife. This threw the trailer to the right and the force snapped the chain holding the plates, which shot sideways off the right-hand side of the lorry. I was just passing him, but they struck my back bumper like a giant guillotine, shearing it in two. If I'd been 10 feet further back, they'd have cut the car in half with me inside.

So, missing a bomb from Hitler by 20 yards and steel from Sheffield by 10 feet, keep your head down, Bernard, and stay lucky!

The summer season was at the Windmill Theatre on Great Yarmouth seafront, a lovely little theatre run by Peter Jay, who also owned the town's circus. The Jay family were proper pros (Peter had even been in the pop charts: remember the Jaywalkers? No neither do I, but they were great people to be around).

The season involved just one performance, at 7.30pm, Monday to Saturday, but there was more to it than that. On Sundays, I'd hoof it up and down to London to do the odd TV like 'Blankety Blank' and every Tuesday after the show would see me haring down the A12 for a Butlins' Midnight Cabaret' in Clacton. That Yarmouth to Clacton run was tight, to say the least. I'd screech up to the Butlins Night Club stage door at half past midnight, the Redcoats would be waiting to unload and set up my props, and 20 minutes later, I'd be onstage for an hour's cabaret followed by an autograph/photo session. Exhausted, the adrenaline alone got me back to Yarmouth, usually around daybreak, disturbing the seagulls as I drove down the prom.

The workload I'm describing was par for the course. I'd do anything, go anywhere on the premise that 'if I don't do it, someone else will'.

FROM MICROLIGHTS TO MARATHONS

On the bill with me at the Windmill was Johnnie Kennedy, not only a great comedian but something of an athlete, running regular marathons. He took me on a few short runs and I became hooked.

Within a few weeks, I was jogging every day and by the time the season ended, I was much fitter.

The first London Marathon had been held earlier in the year and I was very impressed by the Fancy Dress aspect of the event. One costume, in particular, caught my eye: a rhino with two men inside and it got me thinking, if they could do 26 miles inside a rhino, what about me trying 'on an ostrich'.

The more I thought about it, the more interested I became. I was fit, I'd been through my rugby and squash periods, so maybe a marathon was the next big thing for me.

I knew to have any chance I would need a lightweight 'bird'. I was working at Yorkshire TV in Leeds and met the Rowley family. The Rowley's were prop makers who had built the famous Dusty Bin Character, a radio-controlled 'prop' which played a major part in the successful ITV '3-2-1' series, hosted by Ted Rogers.

They were very confident with the 'spec' I gave them and went ahead to 'breed' a featherweight ostrich capable of running a marathon.

The next few months leading up to panto saw me as busy as ever, with one 'gig' I'll never forget. It was a week in Monte Carlo for the car manufacturer British Leyland. They were flying out their dealers by the plane load on three-day 'jollies', the highlight of which was a cabaret evening featuring Yours Truly; the amazing singer Helen Geltzer; and the even more amazing Neville King (a brilliantly funny ventriloquist but, as you'll discover, there was much more to him than that).

We were in the Principality for several days, one night on, one night off. Helen Geltzer, obviously well connected, had turned up in a chauffeur-driven Cadillac stretch limousine. We became friendly with her chauffeur Max and when he offered, we jumped at the chance of an evening out in the 'limo'.

Our party was made up as follows: me, my pianist

Terry Herrington, Neville King and his lady friend and the show's producer, Ernest Maxim, and his wife.

Ernest was a 'Premier League' TV producer, amongst his credits was the "Morecambe and Wise Show".

First stop was a restaurant on the outskirts of town. It was early December and the place was quiet, but not for long. I ought to mention that in the boot of the car was my enormous, padded 'fat suit'. I'd brought it with me (as you do) for a spot of mischief.

Complete with stetson, silk scarf and shades, I became 'Ricardo Monte', the Californian car dealer – owner of the biggest British Leyland franchise on the West Coast.

The meal was hysterical, the staff watched spellbound as Neville made the bread rolls' talk' to each other. He was a genius, regarded by everyone in the business as one of the best' vents'; he even seemed to be able to 'throw' his voice in different directions.

The meal over, I wandered outside and sat in a metal chair on the pavement but because of my girth, I became stuck in my chair and staggered around with it firmly attached to my rear end. A total pantomime...and that was just for starters.

The British Leyland boss was Tony Ball (who had a talented son Michael: yes, that one). We set out to track him down.

The itinerary that evening for the dealers included a visit to the Monte Carlo Sporting Club, where Tony would be hosting a Reception.

I'll now describe what followed, AND IT'S ALL TRUE!

As the Cadillac glided to a halt at the club entrance, Terry and Neville leapt out as my' bodyguards'. They were both wearing dark glasses and each had a hand inside their jackets as if holding a concealed weapon. The two uniformed security guards on the top step immediately disappeared (Why wouldn't they?).

'Ricardo Monte' waddled out of the car to be greeted by a concierge, hovering for a tip. Ricardo pulled out a wad of notes, waved 100 Francs in the air and passed it to Terry, who passed it to Neville, who put it in his top pocket and gave the poor man a pound note!

Pure theatre – and we were making it up by the minute. The whole entourage followed 'Ricardo' into this iconic building. We swept past the gaming tables and the scores of punters, who parted like the waves to let the tour party through.

We could overhear the comments: "Who is he?"

"No idea, but he must be filthy rich."

"Look at her, that blonde at the back," (Neville's Lady), "she looks a right floozie."

'Ricardo' accosted a BL Manager and introduced himself as the 'West Coast Big Cheese'. I told him he was looking for Tony Ball and if he didn't meet him there and then, I was leaving.

The poor man turned pale: "Yes, Mr Monte, I'll try and find him."

"Never mind 'try', son, just find him."

We were through the building like a dose of salts and back in the car quickly while our luck held.

'Ricardo' saw the BL Manager pick up a telephone by his elbow.

"Mr Monte."

He was silenced by a wave of a podgy hand: "What a load of crap, (into the phone), what kind of a tinpot operation are these Brits running? They can't even find this 'Tony Ball' character".

"We're heading for the airport,"I said, putting down the

phone. "If you ever do find this Ball guy, tell him he's missed the boat, Ricardo Monte don't hang around for anybody."

"Sorry, Mr Monte."

He stepped back as we inched forward, just missing the Concierge as the car drove off. We got round the corner and begged Max to stop.

The hysteria could be contained no longer, we fell out of the car, rolling around on the grass verge, panting with laughter.

Remember, it was the early Eighties, when people were more easily impressed.

The car was the key, as first impressions are everything and we had the guts to see it through. It shows how people can be 'conned' by appearances.

You'd never get away with it today...would you?

NEVILLE THE DEVIL

I could write a whole book about Neville King. I've already mentioned his prowess as a ventriloquist, both on and off stage, but there's another story I have to tell.

He was in Canada with a big British variety show. Also on the show was the funniest man I had ever met, Norman Collier. The pair of them would create havoc in hotels, with Neville's skills convincing staff and guests there was someone hiding in the luggage!

One day, Neville was in a hotel gents toilet, standing at the urinal alongside a couple of American guys, when he noticed almost under his nose an air freshener with a round chrome grill. He spoke into the grill.

NEVILLE: "Hello."

(The grill appeared to reply, in a metallic voice),

GRILL: "How may I help you?"

NEVILLE: "I'd like to order breakfast, please."

GRILL: "Yes sir, please place your order."

NEVILLE: "Two eggs, fried, bacon and sausage."

GRILL: "Two eggs, fried, bacon and sausage."

NEVILLE: "Oh, and pancakes and black coffee for two."

GRILL: "Pancakes and black coffee for two."

NEVILLE: "I'll be there in five minutes, thank you."

GRILL: "You're welcome."

Neville zipped up, rinsed his hands, nodded at his dumbstruck neighbours and as he walked out, held the door ajar to hear their conversation...

"Did you see that?"

"I saw it."

"The guy ordered breakfast in the john."

"I heard him."

"Let's try it."

"HELLO, can I get two coffees, (the louder), HELLO, HELLO !"

Sadly Neville and Norman have passed away, and both these giants of comedy are sorely missed.

FROM MONTE CARLO TO MAYHEM

I must have gone down well in Monte Carlo (on stage, I mean) because the boss asked me to stay for a second week for the next influx of dealers. I explained that my panto rehearsals started the very next day in Slough but I would fly back, ask for time off and return in two days.

On this premise, I left all my props backstage and caught a flight to Heathrow.

I booked in at the Holiday Inn just off the M4, as close to Slough as I could get.

Up early, I threw open the curtains to reveal a devastating sight. Overnight there had been some kind of a blizzard and I was gazing down at a Siberian landscape.

I managed to get a cab and slalomed my way to the stage door of the Fulcrum Theatre.

Within minutes, any hopes I was harbouring of going back to Monte Carlo were dashed, as the producer was not a happy bunny. Half the cast hadn't made it, along with most of the scenery, and the weather would put the blocks on the Box Office doing well.

He also told me that business was pretty bad anyway, (as I was top of the bill, he had a look in his eye that said it was all my fault). I tentatively asked about returning to Monte Carlo anyway, but got a very firm NO! (Best if I leave out his actual reply, it ended in "OFF").

So there I was, from the heady delights of Monaco, now marooned in Slough. Nobody could get in or out of the town centre, so the panto was in trouble. To use some of a well-known song title, 'There's no business' (And there was no business!).

We just got on with rehearsals as best we could.

To make matters worse, a few days later, I had a gig in north London. It was a private function and I managed to get there after rehearsals. Amazingly, so did my pianist Terry, who heroically had travelled down from Barnsley. Problem was, all my props, clothes and music were in Monte Carlo.

The band rehearsal proved interesting. Terry scribbled down some arrangements on a few table napkins and I went on, in a sense, naked.

All I had was the clothes I stood up in (and listen to this

for dedication): Terry changed socks with me because his were black and mine were white.

To think, a few days earlier, we'd been cruising around Monaco in a Cadillac and here we were swopping socks.

Somehow I got through the cabaret, but not with flying colours. So, after thanking Terry for going the extra mile (in every sense), I headed back to Slough.

My time in Slough was not a happy one. Business was really bad, as only the brave or foolish would go out in those conditions. I ventured north one Sunday that January for a recording of 'The Good Old Days' at the City Varieties in Leeds and miraculously made it there and back in one piece. The M1 was down to one lane, very hazardous and dangerous, but "the show must go on".

Brave or foolish? (Answers on a postcard!).

WANTED, 80-YEAR-OLD ROADIE

Pantomime over, I rested for a week and then started packing.

I was joining the QE2 in San Francisco for a leg of a world cruise. The deal with Cunard included travel for two (supposedly for my road manager), but I asked my Dad if he fancied it and he said yes.

Danny Quinn had turned 80, but was spritely with it. The oldest roadie in the business was my Dad.

We flew from Manchester, boarded in San Francisco and headed for Sydney. Idyllic times they were, and it was great having the old man on board as we called at various Pacific Islands en route.

I was determined to attempt my first London Marathon two months later, and took the opportunity to get some 'on deck' miles under my belt. It was four laps to a mile and over the years, I would do hundreds and hundreds on that beautiful liner.

Eventually arriving in Sydney, we began the next phase of our world tour.

I'd booked a few weeks' work in the clubs 'down under', and Cunard had paid for the travel.

Aussie audiences were the best, because if they liked you, they let you know it. I had a friend from Chesterfield called Geoff, a telephone engineer, who'd emigrated a couple of years earlier and he kindly gave us the use of his house. Another St Helens emigree lent me his car, so we had it all going for us.

We drove up the Pacific Highway for a week's cabaret in Tweed Heads, which is on the border with Queensland. We stayed at the Cooks Endeavour Motel, a very comfortable place with immaculate gardens; I remember watching the gardener mowing the lawns, then getting down on his knees and trimming the edges with a pair of large scissors.

We had the Barron Knights for company, another British success doing well 'down under'.

I'm so glad I spent that time with my Dad; it was really precious. Now here I am, turned 80, and trying to make sure I do the same with my kids. You can't get that time back!

So pick up the phone, ring round your folks, get together while you can, before it's too late.

Try telling a younger person that 'life is short' and you might see their eyes glaze over, but we 'old uns' know, don't we?

THE EIGHTIES HAVE BEEN GOOD TO ME

Bowing out of the Seventies with the Royal Variety Show should have meant my trajectory upwards would be ever steeper. It didn't happen, but I was still in demand and my workload was staggering, as you'll gather as I take you through this period.

In 1982, I was asked by Thames TV to host a summer spectacular, the 'Big Top Variety Show'. I got Rob Grant and Doug Naylor on board as writers, and I was confident the series would be successful.

The show was staged in Billy Smart's huge circus tent and, like it said on the tin, included a mixture of circus acts and 'turns'. Not any old 'turns' but proper stars: Lulu and Gene Pitney, for a start.

It was a big production with dancers, guest acts and circus performers, who I thought were amazing, especially the family acts from Eastern Europe, including jugglers, tumblers, even knife throwers; they all had a fantastic work ethic.

Often comprising three generations, they would rehearse all day, eat together and then perform as if their lives depended on it. I have the utmost admiration for those people. I still meet up with Ringmaster Norman Barrett when he's in town with Zippo's Circus, and love going backstage to spend time with them.

The variety show was produced and directed by Chris Palmer and, surprisingly, we're good friends to this day.

Surprisingly? Time to read on…

Chris was an experienced TV man but was best known for producing the enormously successful travel show, 'Wish You Were Here', hosted by Judith Chalmers. The variety show was something he did every year, and I know he enjoyed the annual change of direction.

Being on location added to the excitement, as we were housed in a line of caravans. I even heard the dancers complaining in the next-door caravan that they didn't have a fridge to keep their wine cool. I had a fridge, so I went out and bought a large roll of plastic pipe. I wedged one end into a bottle of wine on the top shelf and the other end went into the girl's caravan. Using gravity and considerable lung power, they were able to syphon the 'plonk' into their plastic cups!

A clear example of the saying, 'necessity is the mother of invention' and at the same time, it was hilarious, especially as the 'Syphon Squad' had to get down on their hands and knees to make it work!

Chris Palmer was easygoing with a great sense of humour, and it wasn't long before the mischief started kicking in.

I remember rehearsing a stunt which involved me being suspended on a wire (on an ostrich), 30 feet above the circus ring. They left me up there while they went for lunch!

Then one morning, Chris was checking out of the hotel and was stopped by the hotel porter (at my behest), to have his suitcase opened, revealing a large quantity of sheets and towels I'd crammed in while he was having breakfast!

CHRIS PALMER'S GAS BILL

Here's one of the best examples of mischief I can think of...

I was one of the last to leave rehearsals and noticed a stamped addressed envelope on Chris's desk.

It was his gas bill and he'd forgotten to post it. I took it back to the hotel, steamed it open and wrote the longest rant of a 'complaining' letter that the Thames Gas Board would ever receive.

Totally over the top, it went along the lines of: "I'm paying this bill against my better judgement. This is the last time, though, I know what you're up to, lining your pockets, you greedy fat cats, stacking up profits at my expense. I work hard for a living while you lot sit back and take us for every last penny."

"Well, it's over. I'm forming the 'Worcester Park Don't pay your Gas Bill' movement', and we'll show you. Take a good look at this cheque before you cash it; it's the last you'll get from me."

I put the letter in the envelope along with his cheque, resealed it and popped it in the post.

All the crew were in on it. The following morning, Chris was told the envelope had been seen and posted and the incident was forgotten about…until a few weeks later, during a meeting with the same crew, the subject of utility bills came up and Chris said: "That reminds me, after I paid my gas bill last month, I got this weird letter from Thames Gas. It went on about any profits they made were invested in making sure their customers would receive better service and any non-payment of bills could only result in court action and termination of supply. I've no idea what they were on about".

The whole room collapsed while Chris sat there, completely bemused.

"Why's everyone laughing? What's so funny?"

I must say, though, that when it was explained, he took it in good part.

CHAPTER 13
THE BELGIUM TOURIST BOARD AND THE HILTON HOTEL
(HOW'S THAT FOR A CHAPTER HEADING!)

It was November 28, 1983, and I met my good friend Rusty Goffe in London. Rusty, a talented musician, was a dwarf (and still is). We were going out for a meal while I was in the capital.

I rang Chris Palmer to say hello only to be told that Chris was also 'in town' that evening and as the producer of the 'Wish You Were Here' TV series, was hosting a dinner at the Hilton Hotel for the Belgium Board of Tourism.

Less than an hour later, anyone in Park Lane would have been bemused to see a man, carrying a briefcase, led by a dwarf, entering the Hilton Hotel. (It's perhaps worth mentioning that the briefcase carrier was sitting on an ostrich!).

We convinced security that we had been booked as entertainment and burst into a large private dining room.

I don't want to appear ignorant, but I'd never really thought about the Belgian sense of humour. I knew they were brilliant at making beer and chocolates, but humour: I was about to find out.

Our entrance was greeted with stunned silence by the group of more than 20 Flemish civic dignitaries sat at a large table. The party, I learned later, included the Mayor of Blankenburg, and I mention him only because he was one of those particularly NOT amused!

The only sound was that of Chris Palmer trying to slide under the table whilst stabbing himself to death with a fork and his PA, Mary Hutchinson, stuffing bread rolls in her mouth to stifle the hysterics.

I discovered later that, prior to our entrance, the evening was not going too well and our invasion administered the final coup de grace, as they say when they're incontinent.

Well, we were in the room, and the hush was deafening. I needed to get out, so I repeated the Zsa Zsa Gabor 'gold bars' act that I had done on the Russell Harty show, that I mentioned earlier. As the silence showed no sign of abating, I turned and ran, leaving my accomplice and ostrich handler Rusty Goffe to collect the gold bars and follow me.

Sometime later, when I'd plucked up the courage to phone Mr Palmer, he attempted to take me through that evening.

He confirmed the evening had indeed been 'limping along', but when 'circus surreal' came in, it shuddered to a halt.

One more thing. As I was leaving by the hotel's revolving doors, I bumped into an American who, gaping at the ostrich, said: "That's amazing. I'll give you 500 bucks for him!"

I declined his offer and left.

CHRIS PALMER...ONE MORE TIME!

I continued to 'haunt' Chris, with the help of his crew.

I happened to be in Paignton once at the same time he was there filming (my mole informed me). I invaded his shoot on the back of a nun (don't ask), causing chaos, and then departed quickly before I was asked to leave.

Even better, this one...only a couple of years ago, he invited me to a party at his house in a lovely part of Surrey. The party coincided with the Pope's visit to the UK and the papers were full of his Holiness' picture.

That Sunday afternoon, dressed in the full Pontiff outfit, resplendent from head to toe as the Head Honcho of the Catholic Church, I emerged from my car.

Pausing only to give blessings to his bemused neighbours, I knocked on his front door with my Papal Staff (actually my battered trombone). The look of horror on his face as it opened was worth the hire fee alone!

The reaction from his party guests was a stunned (Belgian) silence, but they eventually came around. The atmosphere wasn't helped by asking them to sing along to some popular hymns while I played the trombone.

A footnote to this...also at the party was my recently departed friend, Ed Stewart. We were both heading for a Water Rats Lodge meeting that evening, and I offered him a lift. I decided to stay in 'Pope Mode', as it would make for a comedy entrance and we like those, don't we?

On the way to Kings Cross, Ed suggested we take a route passing close to Stamford Bridge, unaware that Chelsea were playing at home. As we drove past the stadium, the final whistle went and we were caught up in horrendous traffic, me sitting there at the wheel dressed as the Pope. I'd like to say the comments from the passing fans were merely ribald, but I'm afraid they were much worse.

The last laugh goes to Chris Palmer.: The Big Top Variety Show was disliked by the critics and one, in particular, hated me and wrote a scathing feature, complete with photographs, tearing me apart.

Chris loved it; he couldn't contain his glee. He took the article, had it enlarged and framed and presented it to me with much ceremony.

It still hangs in my kitchen, an ironic yet happy reminder of our times together.

BLACKPOOL BECKONS

A Blackpool summer season is a landmark for many entertainers of my generation, especially if the show is on one of the piers. I remember Ken Dodd saying that if you wanted to pay him a proper compliment, call him an 'End of the Pier' comedian.

I can't improve on that. To walk up the Pier, in all weathers (as Ken Dodd says: 'roped together') and perform to an audience, which often includes three generations of the same family all determined to enjoy themselves, is wonderful and I'm fortunate to have experienced it many times.

In 1983 it was the South Pier that welcomed me along with one of our most talented show groups, the 'Rocking Berries', plus puppeteers, singers and dancers.

It was a proper family variety show and it was right up my street. There was pressure on the length of your spot, so no padding, just the best bits of your act made it.

As it was a resident season, I found it less wearing, no tearing up and down motorways for late-night cabaret dates.

It would have been even less wearing if I'd taken up golf and done nothing else during the day, but no, I was still being bitten by the flying bug so I enrolled at Blackpool Airport for some flying lessons and hopefully get my pilot's licence.

Not a moment too soon, you might think, considering I'd been flying on and off for a couple of years. But things were changing in the world of Microlighting. The cavalier attitude that existed a couple of years earlier was over, now it was being regulated.

Pilot's licence, insurance, medical and an annual 'MOT' for the aeroplane would all become necessary to stay in the air – and a good thing too.

Thinking back, there must have been hundreds of pilots back then who, like me, took to the skies unsupervised, not really knowing what they were doing. I'm grateful to have survived that period and enjoyed half a lifetime of the most amazing experiences anyone can have. To be on your own, at 1,000 feet in an open-air cockpit, chugging along at 50mph is mesmerising and once you've been there, you're hooked forever.

Thanks to Andy Wallbridge, who ran a flying school at the airport, I passed the written exam, then got the required flying hours by doing some cross-country flights to eventually become a fully-fledged, fully-legal Microlight pilot.

THE MENAGERIE FLIES SOUTH

The South Pier Show was going well, six nights a week, and because of my policy of 'don't turn any work down', Sundays became interesting too.

An enterprising producer named Jack Sharpe had come up with a great idea. Why not fill an aeroplane with entertainers who were working in the north during the week and fly them south to Devon on Sundays to work the theatres in Torquay and Paignton.

And so it was, one Sunday morning in July, a motley crew assembled at Blackpool Airport: Roger De Courcey (with Nookie the Bear), Keith Harris (with Orville the Duck and Cuddles the Monkey), and me (with Oswald the ostrich, Justin the cat and an unnamed rubber shark). There was also Stan Boardman, the funny Scouser who almost got Des O'Connor taken off the air with his infamous 'Fokkers' gag, live on TV.

The mayhem started beside the runway when it became clear there would be a problem getting all the performers and their 'animals' in the six-seater Cessna. Eventually, the pilot decided this could only be accomplished by removing one of the seats. This did not go down well with Stan, who had brought his mate along from Scarborough that morning on the promise of a 'jolly' down in Torquay. The outcome was that Stan's pal was left behind while the rest of us squeezed in.

Stan was so funny: "Do you realise," he said, "we've got a duck, a monkey, a bear, a fish, a cat and an ostrich on board. If we crash somewhere out in the country, they'll think we're some kind of flying Safari Park".

We repeated this trip every Sunday during the peak

season. I'm not sure if the sortie was economically viable, but for those on board, it was unforgettable.

One more story about Stan: we met outside the Torquay hotel every Monday morning to be taken by coach to Exeter for the return flight.

On one occasion, there was no sign of Stan. We were running late and there was a possibility we would have to leave without him. He suddenly rolled around the corner bleary-eyed, wearing his suit from the night before. We piled into the coach and set off.

It was a blazing hot morning, and the rest of us were dressed suitably in shorts and T-shirts. As the coach crawled along the seafront in heavy traffic, Stan rummaged in his holdall and found his T-shirt and shorts. He stripped to the buff, ignoring the groans from his fellow travellers. As he struggled to put the T-shirt over his head, I picked up his discarded Y-fronts and flung them out of the open door of the coach onto the street.

"You bastard," he yelled, "they cost me a bloody fiver."

With no further ado, he leapt off the coach and, naked apart from a T-shirt and socks, raced back down the road and recovered his underwear. Bowing to the crowd on the pavement, he shouted, "sorry, no autographs, folks" and got back on the coach.

We were all convulsed, laying on the floor in hysterics.

That's Stan Boardman.

ANOTHER YEAR, ANOTHER PANTO

This time it was the Theatre Royal, Nottingham, a beautiful theatre designed by the great Frank Matcham, and a great space to perform in.

The panto was 'Dick Whittington', and it was a first-class production with a great cast headed by Little and Large, along with Julie Rogers, magician Geoffrey Durham (aka the Great Soprendo), Joe Black and me, plus several baby ostriches ridden by children from a local dance school. Also in the cast with a non-speaking part was a young Brian Conley (yes, that one).

During the run, I was booked to do Marti Caine's TV show, recorded on a Sunday in London at the BBC.

I'd seen an old piano routine that had been filmed years ago in black and white that I fancied rehashing. I discussed my idea with the legendary Bobby Warans, the BBC props man.

He found me an 'empty' grand piano – just the box with no innards. Bobby not only found it but sent it up to Nottingham in a van so I could rehearse. I recruited our panto fairy, Sue Stevens, and we practised the routine between shows. It was hard work but would be worth it.

The plan was that, earlier in the TV show, I would do a brief crossover behind Marti, apparently being given a piggyback by a nun. I'd make some reference to the Sound of Music and exit left.

Then in my main spot, I'd be discovered seated at the piano playing (actually miming) the 'Warsaw Concerto'. As I played, the camera would see my fingers being mirrored by the highly polished back surface of the keyboard. (Stay with me, nearly there).

After a couple of dramatic runs up and down the keyboard, the 'mirrored fingers' would develop a mind of their own and become disconnected from my own fingers. I then jumped up and pulled out from the piano the owner of the fingers. (Yes, you've guessed THE NUN, played by Sue Stevens, who then smacked me round the head with her handbag). And boy, did she smack me!

I think that true story tells you what lengths I would go to for a five-minute TV spot.

What it doesn't tell you is how, the following day, when we turned up back in pantoland, I had the most wonderful black eye, the result of being hit with a nun's handbag.

Oh, how I tormented Sue by drawing her attention to my disfigurement during the next few days. She was guilt-ridden, but I wouldn't let it go. Then miraculously, on the third day, she looked at it and realised the injury had changed sides, now it was the other eye that was black.

That's right, I'd been using make-up to get a 'phantom' injury. She still hasn't forgiven me!

1984, SUMMER ON THE ISLAND

My next summer season would be at the Sandown Pavilion Theatre on the Isle of Wight.

I learned later I'd got the job because, on a Sunday off the previous year, I'd driven from Blackpool to the island for a one-night stand (Blackpool to IOW, round trip of 400 miles). Anyway, the round trip was obviously worth it, they liked what they saw that night and booked me for the following summer!

I still had my annual London Marathon to complete, which took place just before the Sandown rehearsals started. Following the publicity the marathon generated, I got a last-minute call from Des O'Connor to appear on his TV show. This would mean my missing the Sandown dress rehearsal. I convinced the promoter Nick Thomas that being on the telly with Des would be good for the summer show and up to London I went, leaving a 'stand in' for the dress and technical rehearsals.

The 'stand in' was Roger the Roadie.

I'd known Roger Hendry for years and he'd become a vital part of my travelling circus. Roger knew my act better than I did. He'd previously been 'company manager' for Hinge and Bracket but, when we got together, he immediately became 'Roger the Roadie', a title he owns to this day, although in recent years he shares the glory with his wife, Debbie.

Roger is not only 'Top Roadie', he's also a talented prop maker, known throughout the business as one of that rare breed who can turn their hand to anything.

There aren't many, but I've met the best: Bill King, Peter Pullon, Roger Hendry.

Backstage geniuses, all of them, as without them, the business wouldn't work.

I once flew with Roger to Paris for a one-nighter. It was a TV Show from the Moulin Rouge, where else!

We arrived backstage at 't'Red Windmill' to be surrounded by lots of stunning female dancers. Or were they showgirls? Did it matter? They were all about 6ft tall and wearing ostrich feathers on their heads, which made them seem even taller. Oh yes, one more thing, they were all topless!

Well, while me and Roger were vying for the title 'English Man with the most Poppy Out Eyes', they were shimmying around us in a confined space and we didn't know where to look. Well we did, but we daren't.

But as we wallowed in the midst of this exotic scene, one of them turned to the other and, in a thick Yorkshire accent you could cut with a knife, said: "Eh, Tracey, yer bugger, av yew still got me eyeliner". Spell broken!

I don't remember much else about the trip, apart from the moment at the airport as we were trying to depart. Our large props trunk was causing a problem, and they wanted to send it later by cargo. We were having none of that so, in an attempt to reveal the contents, we showed the staff a photograph of myself riding the ostrich. This evoked the immortal phrase: "MON DIEU, FORMIDABLE!"

Right, it's back to the ferry heading for Portsmouth to be on telly with Des O'Connor. Meanwhile, back on the IOW at the Sandown Pier Theatre, Roger was doing my dress rehearsal. I never saw his performance, of course, but I was told it was hilarious. He meticulously went through my act with a fine toothcomb, telling every gag and using every prop.

He must have been good because the following day (our opening show), all my lighting, sound and music cues were spot on.

It was such a happy Summer. I shared top billing with Janet Brown during the peak season but, for the whole summer, I was working with my best pals, in no particular order:

• Keith and Alan Simmons (the comedy duo, the 'Simmons Brothers'). They used big props. My kind of act and definitely my kind of people… and still best friends.

(Alan has since done his own 'vent' act and Keith is now a writer and director and tours with his son Ben as the 'Simmons').

• Kenny Martyn, musician, keen angler, a wizard in the kitchen and award-winning glider pilot. There's nothing he can't do! (Kenny now lives in France so I'm sure he's an award-winning multi-linguist by now!).

• Hilary O'Neil, an impressionist, singer and dancer, and a legend in our business. Hilary knows EVERYBODY – and EVERYBODY loves Hilary.

We came up with a title for Hilary's next book, the

'HONDA':

H...ilary

O

N...eil

D...irectory of

A...quaintances.

It's 35 years since we were all listening to Hils doing her act through the backstage tannoy. During the song, 'I'll go where the music takes me', Hilary went for the top note and on the word 'KEY', her voice completely cracked.

A roar went up from us all and we thundered downstairs to the side of the stage, making sure she could see us. With a felt tip pen on a large white card we'd drawn a large KEY, broken in half.

We waved the card gleefully (as we did every night for the rest of the summer) when she went for that note.

You couldn't write this kind of nonsense. It just happens spontaneously between people who love what they're doing and who they're doing it with.

I've spent time telling you about this period, because friendships were forged that last to this day. It's another way of reminding myself what a lucky boy I've been.

We see each other rarely these days. Sadly, we're more likely to meet at funerals but, even then, there's joy in recalling our very own 'Good Old Days".

MEANWHILE, IN DERBYSHIRE

The Sandown summer show ran from Monday for four nights, so on Thursday after the show, we would rush for the 23.59 ferry to Portsmouth, followed by the long drive home.

The few days off also gave me and my family time to continue the quest for a move out of town and we came across a derelict smallholding with outbuildings and some land, not too far from our present house and, crucially, not too remote.

It was just off the beaten track, a perfect location that would suit all the family, but it was a real mess, hadn't been lived in for years, but I thought, "now or never, this is it", and we went for it.

This involved a bidding process I'll describe as a 'Blind Auction'. It went like this...

I'd ring the Agent and make a bid. Then I'd ring the following day to be told he'd had a higher bid. I then raised my bid, only to be told the following day he'd had a higher bid – and so it went on until, a fortnight later, we'd exceeded the original valuation by 25%.

I still don't know if there were other bidders or whether we were being played along, but I didn't care. I'd hired a professional valuer, Stuart McDonald, and he thought I'd gone mad. In fact, his response every time I told him the stakes had risen was "BLUDDY HELL".

It became known as 'BLUDDY HELL FARM', but I was desperate not to miss out.

Eventually, I got the news, it was ours. BLUDDY HELL!

Madge popped round and paid a small deposit to secure the deal, then all I had to do was find a way of borrowing an astronomical amount of cash. I was entering financial territory I'd never even heard of, but nevertheless kept on going.

Before the deal, we were told we had to meet the owner to see if we would 'pass muster'. In other words, it wasn't enough that we had the money to buy (we hadn't, but that was our secret), we needed to convince her that we were suitable neighbours (she lived just down the lane).

I'd describe her as being 'Landed Gentry', a proper country lady. She was (I would discover) an amazing woman, an elderly spinster who lived alone, with many cats in an adjacent rundown farm, although not as rundown as the one I was buying.

We took advice on how to behave and Madge and I went along with Tracy, then 19, who talked about horses and stuff, which must have worked because a few days later, we got the nod.

CHAPTER 14
WHO'S A FARMER THEN?
(CERTAINLY NOT ME!)

It said farm on the gate, but that's as far as it went. Thinking back, I don't think it had a gate, just a gap where a gate had once swung. It was uninhabitable but we set to, albeit with a limited budget, and gradually got it cosy.

It took eighteen months of hard graft before we could move in. When the day of the move arrived, it turned out to be farcical. To save money, instead of hiring a professional removal firm, I'd recruited friends and family. I had my own van and I phoned a Man with a Van cos I'd heard he was cheap. He arrived with his assistant, and it was obvious they weren't up for it.

The man was, how shall I put it, 'slight of build'. It didn't auger well after he'd had a look round, to hear him groan: "You didn't tell me you had a bloody piano".

An even more surreal moment: together with 'Van Man', I was trying to manhandle a settee through the back door when Tracy came running out and shouted "Dad, Des O'Connor's on the phone".

This guy's face was a picture!

The good news was that there was so much work, but I was up for it. The big car had to go. At one stage, we were down to a Ford Escort and a big van but we got through. I look at the place today and think, "won't it be great when it's finished."

As I said earlier, I had a mantra, "Don't turn any work down", and I never did.

Whatever, Wherever it was, I was up for it.

A THESPIAN? MOI!

Early in 1985, Richard Armitage had an idea that might change my life. For years I'd been charging around the country with considerable success, doing okay with plenty of TV guest appearances, even tearin' up on the cruises and in Australia, but I hadn't really broken through to the next level.

How about becoming a comedy actor? I felt I had it in me. It was happening to my contemporaries. People like Russ Abbott, Bobby Knutt, Duggie Brown and Paul Shane had made the move, so why not give it a try?

Dick Ray was producing a stage version of the 'Mating Game' that summer at the Gaiety Theatre in the Isle of Man. The thought of appearing in a well-known farce alongside proper actors appealed to me. There was just one snag, the money was awful.

At a time in my life when I needed every penny, I was being offered a pithy salary to tread the thespian boards.

I took it. I had no option really, as these chances don't come around very often and perhaps a change in direction was just what I needed.

So there I was aboard the ferry heading for Douglas. I'd managed to hang on to my old MGB, which would be an ideal run-around for the island's roads, and I rented a house on the edge of town. So there I was, a 50-year-old fledgling ACTOR.

I have to say my fellow 'thesps' were very kind to me, perhaps respecting the fact that I went into rehearsals knowing my lines. I was word-perfect, which raised the odd eyebrow, but I had to let them know I was serious.

'Eyebrow raising' brings me to our director, Jimmy Thompson, a charming man who was very easy to work with. He told me that when he became a comic actor (and he was brilliant), he would concentrate on 'close-up' work. The first thing he did was to develop the range of his facial expressions. He had the most 'mobile' of faces I'd ever seen; he could do it all – nose wrinkling and lip curling – but, best of all, he could raise his eyebrows individually.

I tried it, but I failed. However, I found this glimpse into the workings of the actor's craft very interesting.

The discipline was difficult for me. In my world of cabaret (and even pantomime), I had free rein, I'd always been given licence to wander off script for the sake of a laugh but on stage, with two or three other actors, you have to be 'on the mark'. They are waiting for you to give them their cue and if they don't get it, they don't like it – and why should they? As ever, a curve to be learned.

The season was going along fine, the island was lovely and took me back to my holidays there when as a teenager. I'd watch the Joe Loss Orchestra at the Villa Marina, especially their singers, Larry Gretton, Rose Brennan and Ross McManus (Elvis Costello's Dad).

I'd see them on stage and think: "Oh, if only that was me". More than thirty years later and what do you know – it WAS me.

I was still short of money, though. My van was parked

I'm on the left, without me wig

Anyone for tennis?

Inflation! It's everywhere

City variety Leeds, where it all started

Long lost cousins

Move over Robbie and Barry

Crackerjack lives on

Ooh, look at the frocks

Mixing with the Richardson's

Mmm, which one of you
went over the top?

Will the chair turn?

Eat your greens. Lots of cabbage, but Jan's the queen

Anita and me

Who came first?

Vegas Jacket for the bin? Never! (Wrong colour)

Thumbs up with Bradley

Come out Bobby, we can see your feet!

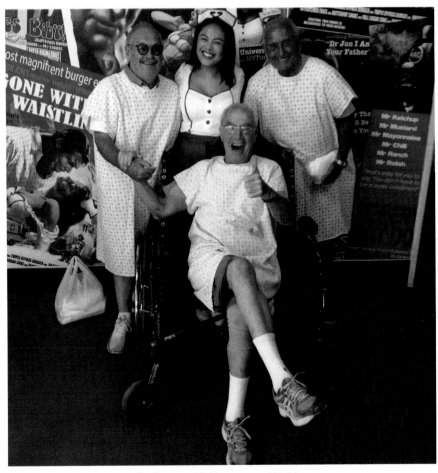

In Vegas with Tommy and Bobby

With Anita and the telly girls

Old man on an old wall

His holiness blesses you

With Paul O'Grady.
For the love of dogs (and ducks!)

Two men, two ducks and Peter Kay

A couple of chuckles

at Blackpool Airport and many a Sunday would see me fly over, then drive to God knows where for a gig.

Verdict on the acting? It didn't really work. It was okay but wouldn't lead to anything. But I'm glad I took the chance, otherwise you never know, do you? Don't die wondering!

CHAPTER 15
BACK TO REALITY

THE winds of change blew through the world of comedy in the early eighties. Winds – more like a hurricane. Comedy became very political. The Thatcher government alienated so many of the younger generation and then along came 'alternative' comedy.

It certainly was different. Gone were the sharp suits, the frilly shirts, mother-in-law jokes and a song to finish. The comics now walked in off the street and went on as they were. T-shirt, trainers and ripped jeans was the look and the previous generation (mine) was taking a hammering, looking really 'past it'.

There was such a sharp divide between the 'now and the then'.

Most of my crowd looked at the new boys and hated them. They looked at us and dismissed us as dinosaurs. There really was animosity between the two factions.

I escaped the worst of it, probably because a lot of what I did was 'off the wall' and unpredictable. But truth to tell, I had a sneaking admiration for their courage.

No props, no music, certainly no jokes. To go out front with nothing but a stream of thought, expand it and make it funny...very brave!

Like it or lump it, change was on the way.

A perfect example is Ross Noble. Go see him live. He'll pick up on the most innocuous incident and turn it into something surreal and always very, very funny. Genius!

Comedy has always changed and always will. I remember, back in 1970, working with a very well-known, successful variety comedian, Bob Andrews. It was a private function somewhere in the Midlands. He did his spot, a gentle mix of stories which went down really well.

Then it was my turn: I came on, exploding onto the stage with my menagerie of animals and inflatable props, and brought the house down.

Bob said afterwards: "Well done, I've learnt something tonight."

I didn't understand what he meant, but I do now. A seasoned veteran, he'd seen another generation arrive, doing stuff in a different way.

A dozen years later, it was happening again: out with the old, in with the new.

Change is inevitable. So what next?

In spite of the new 'wave', fortunately, I was always busy. Summer seasons, pantos, lots of cruising, too. I became a fixture on the QE2 and found I had an advantage, being visual in front of an international audience broke through any language barrier.

The 'ostrich' spot never failed. The Yanks loved it. I was such an athlete back then and with the bird in fifth gear, their reaction was sensational.

I remember jogging on deck the day after I'd performed

and came up alongside Burt Bacharach, who was jogging with a friend.

His friend then asked him: "Hey, Burt, do you know who this guy is?"

"No, who?"

"It's the limey on the chicken!"

The limey on the chicken: I'll settle for that any day!

On one of his jogs, Burt stopped by the table tennis table where I was playing my son David, then 13. I gave the world-famous songwriter my bat, but David was NOT impressed and said: "Who's this, I was ahead!"

I made many great friends on board, friendships that have blossomed down the years. The 'Toaduffs', for example. They were a fantastic song and dance act and were loved by QE2 audiences. Jackie and Roy performed real Broadway-style productions, always to a standing ovation, then just when you thought you'd seen it all, Jackie, a former world champion clog dancer, would jump on a table and dance his socks off.

My times spent on QE2 were precious. In many ways, that liner defines my career and I always feel nostalgic when I visit Dubai to see her berthed in the harbour. I was fortunate enough to be given a private tour a couple of years ago. I say fortunate, but spending time in the cabaret rooms and seeing them deserted was quite an emotional experience.

Happily, she's been converted into a beautiful floating hotel, so a new generation is on board, savouring her delights.

ABSENT FRIENDS

Remembering those 'golden' years, I need to pause and reflect on the joy I've been lucky to share along the way. There have been many special times. Here's just one instance...

Every Thursday, a crowd of us would turn up for breakfast at the lovely Chantry Hotel in Dronfield. The hotel was bought by Jackie and Roy some forty years ago and it became a regular haunt for people both in and out of show business. Following the meal, we would all retire to the lounge for the 'quiz' organised by that unique Octogenarian Comedian, Bobby Dennis. I say 'organised', but it was anything but. Bobby would sit up all night and turn up on the day with a set of complicated questions he could barely pronounce and his audience could hardly comprehend.

He was heckled unmercifully by the whole room, including Sheffield's own Comedian/Actor, the multi-talented Bobby Knutt.

Bizarrely in the midst of this hilarious debacle, the manager, Stuart, would emerge from the kitchen, stop the show and enquire to one and all, "Have you all paid for your tea?".

The party would then move to the lounge with maestro, Terry Herrington on Grand Piano for an hour of unmissable entertainment, performed by a variety of talented people. There are far too many to list, but here are a few.

Jimmy Patton with some wonderful heartwarming stories, Bobby himself as Compere and often Roy, in his 80's but still in tremendous voice. Lots more 'Turns' (as we like to be called) would stand up and perform.

The show would be closed by Jackie, often with the Song, 'I won't send Roses' from the musical 'Mack and Mabel'. Then finally, the whole room would link arms to sing 'We'll Meet Again'.

But here's the thing, they've all sadly passed away. Moved on, I like to think, to that piano lounge in the sky, where one day, we will all 'meet again'. Only a few weeks ago, I was asked by Michael, who has brilliantly managed The Chantry in recent years, if I would do the eulogy at Jackie's funeral. It was an honour to be able to pay tribute to the man, not only a superb entertainer but a special friend.

Along with those already on this page, Jackie Boy, we miss you.

EIGHTIES TO NINETIES

Well, I was certainly as busy in the Nineties, if not busier.

With the era of resident summer seasons ending, the only way of staying in work was to chase it by embarking on a summer of one-night stands.

I recently turned out my diaries from that period, and had I been a lorry driver, the mileage I covered would have been illegal. The Tachometer would have been in permanent meltdown!

In fact, my overriding memory of being on the road during the eighties and nineties is the amount of mileage covered week after week.

PIG'S HEAD IN MINEHEAD

The Butlins Holiday Centres (they dropped the word 'camps' when they went upmarket) always boasted at least one large cabaret venue holding upwards of a 1,000-strong audience. I would headline a weekly 'Midnight Cabaret' there. The show would comprise dancers and one, maybe two, support acts.

I'd go on last, around 1 am and do an hour.

It was energy-sapping, but I was just right for it: plenty of visual gags, lots of audience participation and a couple of big power ballads to finish.

As the season got underway and we got to know our fellow performers, the pranks would start – and here's a couple of examples.

1. As the dancers were onstage, immediately prior to my entrance, we'd be busy sowing the curtains together, thereby blocking their only means of exit.

They would finish a high-energy routine in a "TADARRRR" pose, take the applause, get to their feet and head upstage for a well-choreographed exit: except they couldn't get off, they'd be scrabbling and clawing at the drapes in the most undignified manner.

The rest of us, having regressed to schoolboys, thought it was hysterical, and I have to say that the girls took it well.

2. Performing with us in Minehead that summer were the 'Caravelles', two girls who'd had a big hit with the song 'You don't have to be a Baby to Cry' a few years earlier. We all got on really well, and as we passed a butcher's on Minehead High Street one day, saw something that might help us test the bonds of our friendship. There, snout in the air, was a pig's head.

We got backstage before the girls arrived and placed the head, AKA 'Porky', in the bowl of their toilet and closed both lids. Porky was positioned snout up and, for effect, had an apple in his mouth. A lapel microphone was placed adjacent to the bowl.

Fading up the mic level to 'max' on our mixer desk, we sat and waited.

At five minutes to midnight, the gentle hum of conversation and background music in the cabaret room was suddenly shattered by an ear-piercing scream, as one of the girls lifted the toilet lid.

She emerged from the loo a babbling wreck and in no fit state to stand up, let alone perform. The show was put back while she was plied with brandy and coffee and eventually, like a good pro would, went on with her partner to do their act.

The girls were tall and very attractive, and they maximised their looks by dressing very sexily for the stage, both wearing plunge-neck, clinging sheath gowns which were slit up to the thigh.

Their performance that night had gone down very well. Now fully recovered from the earlier trauma, they were announcing their last song. As they were halfway through the introduction, a man wearing a white coat passed in front of them, literally under their noses.

Was he a waiter, perhaps? (No, it was ME).

On his shoulder, the shoulder nearest the stage, he was carrying a large cardboard box. As he passed beneath them, he opened the lid of the box, revealing to the girls (AND THEM ALONE), the contents!

It was 'PORKY' (who else?).

The effect on the girls was devastating.

One second, glamorous, sexy and the next, gabbling and literally on their knees.

The audience, totally unaware of what was occurring, were baffled. In the early hours of the following morning, I was leaving for the four-hour drive home in my own car, with Peter and Mike behind me in the van.

I took Porky with me, and exited via the main gate on the Promenade. I parked a few yards down and, taking Porky, made my way down onto the deserted beach.

Directly opposite the main gate, I hauled myself up the sea wall and pointed Mr P at the gates, knowing that in a few minutes, as my team left, they couldn't fail to see him in their headlamps. I waited and waited but, unbeknown to me, they had left by another gate!

I scrambled up onto the prom to be accosted by security. I lamely gave my reasons for being there to be greeted by blank stares and head shakes.

I was allowed to leave and a few hours later, when the stench in the car became unbearable, I parted company with Mr P, placing him reverently in a field adjacent to the A38 near Burton on Trent.

The things farmers find on their land, eh:

"You'll never guess what I found in our far field this mornin' ".

I have scores of similar stories. Of jokes played, by me and against me, but if I included them all it would become a Book of Japes, nothing more than an unending list of practical jokes. Maybe that's another book?

I also appreciate that many people don't like practical jokes. They tend to be cruel and require a victim.

My point in including the ones I have are to illustrate the way many of us behaved. It was just the way things were.

MARK RATTRAY, FINE SINGER, FINE JACKET

The incident of Mark Rattray's jacket and the events that led up to it continue to shine a light on MY way of surviving a hectic lifestyle.

It starts at the Bodwellydn Castle Hotel and cabaret venue in North Wales.

I was doing my 'turn' there one night and went into a 'cod' version of 'Singing in the Rain' involving an eccentric Gene Kelly impression. During the dance routine, I felt that my left shoe was working loose. As I continued with my' wacky dance', I thought wouldn't it be funny if I flipped the shoe off my foot as if by accident?" I tried, a couple of times, without success, but I persevered and gave one last mighty flick of the foot. To my horror, the shoe soared away into the darkness over the heads of the audience, most of who were dining.

Have you heard people say when describing an accident 'how everything went into slow motion'? Well, that's exactly how it was. The size ten shoe curled upwards and onwards, high into the gloom above the unsuspecting diners.

KERRASH: the shoe landed on the middle of a table of four people towards the back of the room with a sickening crash. This was followed by a deafening silence from a room full of people: ooh, awkward!

The room remained in stunned silence, so what could I possibly do to recover from this?

I remember shouting, "Waiter, over here… ASAP", but the staff ignored me.

I felt the cold sweat of fear bathe me from head to foot, and then survival clicked in. I looked around and saw that four people on a ringside table had just had a bucket of champagne delivered to them.

I yelled: "Let's play changing tables."

With superhuman strength, fuelled by fear, I picked up the whole 'carnage table' – complete with crockery, smashed glasses, spilt drinks and a size ten shoe – and dragged it over to the 'champagne' table, then swapped the two tables.

Regaining my composure, I then served the stolen champagne to the 'carnage' victims, hauled a hapless waiter over to the ringside table and ordered him to bring them more champagne and then simply got on with my act. Incredibly, I got away with it.

The rest of the show went well. I met the 'victims' later and they didn't seem to mind one bit, something for them to dine out on in later life!

As a result of that evening, I had a great rapport with the staff. Having coffee with them the following morning, one of them even asked me if the 'shoe business' was always in the act.

That was the morning that marked the beginning of the saga of Mark Rattray's jacket. Mark was a great singer and the owner of a very expensive leather jacket.

We'd worked together in panto and were good mates.

During the panto at the Swan Theatre High Wycombe (Dick Whittington, if you must know, starring Lucy Benjamin, Kate O'Mara, me and Mark), Mark, as was the custom, changed characters during the interval from the ship's captain to the Sultan of Morocco.

To cheer the rest of us up – and hopefully 'corpse' us all – he would make his first entrance as the Sultan wearing varying shades of make-up and different, sometimes outrageous, moustaches.

And so time passed, and there I was at the reception of Bodwellydn Castle enjoying a coffee, when someone asked if I knew Mark Rattray.

"Of course, he's a good friend of mine. Why?"

"Well, he appeared here last week and left his leather jacket behind."

Kerching (That's the sound of mischief appearing on the horizon!).

"Lucky for him," I lied, "I'm seeing him next week and I'll drop it off. Tell you what, why don't we phone him to confirm what we are doing."

His home number was produced, and a few moments later I was speaking to him, not in my own voice, of course, but in a cross between Kenneth Williams and Roger Moore.

"Mr Rattray."

"Speaking."

"Ah, Mr Rattray, glad we've tracked you down. My names Henry Yardley, and I'm calling from Bodwellydn Castle in North Wales."

"Oh, yes."

"I'm afraid I'm the bearer of bad news, Mr Rattray. In the early hours of this morning, there was a fire in the backstage area of the cabaret room."

"A fire? Oh my God, was anyone hurt?"

"Thankfully no, but there was considerable damage to the dressing room, which is why I'm calling you. I'm the insurance assessor for the Warners holiday group and I believe you left an item of clothing in the dressing room."

"Oh no, not my leather jacket, my best designer leather jacket."

"I'm afraid so. Anyway, it's my job to make a list of all

the items in the room in order to make a claim. I wonder if you could give me an idea of the value of the jacket."

"I don't believe it, my best leather jacket. Well, it cost over three hundred pounds."

"I beg your pardon?"

"Yes, three hundred pounds."

(Me, incredulously): "Three hundred pounds?"

(Mark, losing it): "Yes, three hundred pounds, it's a designer label."

(Me again, even more incredulous and enjoying this beyond belief): "Three…Hundred…Pounds? Well, I'm sorry, Mr Rattray, but under the conditions of the policy, the maximum value to be paid out per article is thirty pounds."

(Mark's turn to be incredulous): "Thirty pounds, I'm not having that. I mean, I spoke to your Entertainments Manager and he said he would post it to me."

"Entertainments Manager? We haven't got an Entertainments Manager."

"You have, I spoke to him yesterday."

"Ah, yesterday, that was before the fire. I'm afraid he's been sacked as he was enjoying a cigar last night backstage, left the stub alight and caused the fire. Fortunately, he was unharmed, but he had to go."

Me again: "While we are talking, Mr Rattray, I have a memo from head office that concerns you. It says that from this date you are barred from performing at any Warners' holiday venue because of the inappropriate behaviour in your act."

"Inappropriate: What do you mean?"

"Inappropriate and perhaps even racial."

"Well, Mr Rattray, let me quote from the memo…in one

of your appearances, you were seen to insult the Moroccan Royal Family with a false moustache."

There was a long, long pause…then the penny began to drop for Mark.

I finally relented and revealed my identity.

"Clifton, you are a complete b*****", and many expletives later: "I might have known it was you."

I must say he took it very well. We ended the call as friends and I promised to post his jacket back to him without delay.

But I'm afraid to say that the mischief genie wouldn't go back in his bottle, as I kept the jacket for a while. Everywhere I went, the jacket went too, along with my camera, and whenever I met someone remotely famous, I took a photo of them wearing the jacket and, some weeks later, I had a collection of photos including Jim Bowen, Kathy Staff, Tom O'Connor, Fatima Whitbread, Mike Smith plus Ollie, my bearded collie dog, and finally Zigga, my daughter's horse.

The first envelope to drop through Mark's letter box contained a photograph and a letter that went something like this…

Dear Mr Rattray,

My name is Jim Bowen, you may have heard of me. I was recently on a cruise with a Mr Bernie Clifton and bought a leather jacket from him which, as you can see, I am wearing in the photograph I have enclosed.

The reason I am writing is that he told me you once owned this jacket, and as I intend to insure it against loss or theft, I need to know its value. Perhaps you would be kind enough to tell me how much it's worth. Thus far, estimates vary from £30 to £300.

Thanking you in anticipation of an early reply.

Yours,

Jim Bowen.

Over the next few weeks, it was followed by similar letters, ostensibly from the aforementioned celebrities, Kathy Staff, Fatima Whitbread, Tom O'Connor, etc., although the text was considerably different from Ollie the collie and Zigga the pony!

Mark's reaction to the correspondence was at first positive, but then changed as the process continued until even I had to agree that enough was enough and, in order to preserve our friendship, promised to return the jacket to him. This I did, but had to send it by courier and the irony was not lost on me when I had to state its value for insurance purposes!

That, I thought, was the end of this saga, until one Sunday evening a few months later. On my way back from a gig, I was driving through St Albans, passing close to the St Albans Arena, the local theatre. As I stopped at the lights, my attention was drawn to a large billboard.

TONIGHT, LIVE ON STAGE, SONGS FROM THE SHOWS

Starring Mark Rattr...

I never finished reading. I swung the car around and, a few minutes later, I was inside the theatre talking to the manager, who was known to me.

She confirmed that Mark was appearing there that evening and that he was on stage performing his set.

She escorted me backstage to his dressing room on the premise that, as I was a friend of his, it would be okay to wait there for him until the end of the show.

As I entered the room, I had to rub my eyes in disbelief. There, draped over the back of a chair, was THE JACKET!

Well, thank you, God.

A few minutes later, I was standing at the back of the auditorium listening to Mark's beautiful rendition of a medley from the 'Student Prince'.

I was carrying an ice bucket containing a bottle of champagne (empty actually), and I was wearing, you've guessed it, the jacket.

As the song ended, I set off down the aisle towards the stage.

Mark was taking the applause when he saw what he thought was a fan bringing him champagne, he bent down to receive it but then recognised me, which kind of floored him. He spluttered for bit, then recovered slightly, but when he noticed the jacket, it really finished him off. He went totally 'gaga'. I shook hands and made my way back through the audience.

Mark then attempted to compose himself but, in buying himself some time, made the mistake of trying to explain the situation to the audience, but only succeeded in bemusing them. However, he recovered, finished his show, met me later in his dressing room and shook me warmly by the throat.

NB. It's worth saying that Mark has since changed his life dramatically (hopefully not as a result of the episode you've just read). Originally, he was working as an orthopaedic nurse when he went on Opportunity Knocks (and won it), so he gave up the medical profession and entered show business as a full-time entertainer. He subsequently appeared on the Royal Variety Performance and starred in more than 200 sell-out dates in 'The Magic of The Musicals'. However, he decided to go back to his first love and can often be seen as a real-life paramedic on Channel 4.

BREAKFAST WITH MONICA

When it came to touring in the 80s and the 90s, THE most important question was, "Where will we sleep?" There were hotel options, but they were expensive and didn't cater for the lifestyle kept by 'Professional Entertainers', which is why we always went for 'Pro Digs' (accommodation for 'Pros'). We'd often get in late after our show, and the following morning, we would need a very late breakfast. Like any form of business, there were good, bad and indifferent examples... and Monica. I've picked the most interesting.

Let me take you to Southampton. I'd booked a week of Social Clubs in and around the city for agents Les and Myrtle Osman. Having asked about 'digs', they gave me Monica's number, so I booked in for the week. The first show had gone well; I looked up Darwin Road on my road map and turned up around midnight. As it happened, I'd twisted my ankle earlier in the day and was walking with a pronounced limp. Within 5 minutes of arriving at the house, I found myself in the front room with a cup of cocoa, my foot immersed in a bowl of hot water, all arranged by this force of nature called Monica, a lady in her 60s who, I was to learnt, never took "No" for an answer. Along with the cocoa and ankle therapy I was given a 'snack', (Monica's description), which turned out to be half a loafs worth of cheese on toast. My stagger upstairs was more down to the humungous supper than my sprained ankle.

I slept soundly, and around eleven the following morning, I went downstairs for the "anytime you like" breakfast. Thirty years later, I still remember. Within seconds of sitting down, Monica had delivered a large pot of tea to the table. As the only one in the dining room, I was taken aback when it was followed by a few rounds of toast and bacon with the words, "Just to keep you going". I say 'the only one in the dining room', but during this time, I was conscious of being watched intently by the baleful eye of a large grey parrot swaying on its perch. While I was working my way through the 'first' course, I discovered that Monica and her husband Ron had spent many years in Kenya, before returning to settle in Southampton. I was also about to learn that the Swahili word for 'Cat' was 'Paca'. Is this relevant? Read on.

Halfway through my mug of tea, Monica spotted a neighbour's cat in the garden. "PACA, PACA, PACA!" She shouted. Immediately, a posse of small dogs emerged at speed from the front room, yapping furiously as they headed for the back door, which conveniently had been left open. The circus continued in the garden as they vainly chased their (now disappeared) prey. Eventually, the dogs, looking really pleased with themselves, returned to 'Base Camp' while Monica explained, "PACA, PACA". She'd had a few dogs in Kenya and that was the local 'shout' to rid the garden of undesirables, not just cats, but the occasional monkey. As calmness descended back at the table, the main course was slid under my nose. This included more bacon, almost hidden by a brace of fried eggs, black puddings and what else but a mountain of beans. I was totally stuffed and had to take a turn around the block, eventually sitting on a wall for a while to recover. So that was it, my very first 'Monica Breakfast', memorable, eh? But wait till you hear about the next one...

The following morning, I was halfway through my mound of eggs, bacon, beans etc, when the parrot (remember him) became very agitated, and instead of his usual 'cluck, cluck, clucking', demonstrated his gift of mimicry. "PACA, PACA, PACA", he clucked. "PACA, PACA, PACA". Immediately, the 'PACA Patrol' at full throttle entered from the front room and crossed the kitchen, heading for the garden. At the same time, the parrot saw his chance, launched himself from his perch and landed on my bacon. I recoiled in horror as he grabbed a rasher and flew back to his perch. Bedlam! Dogs yapping, parrot clucking, me gurgling. Monica then charged in, cornered the thief and 'urged' him into his cage, which is where he stayed for the rest of my visit (perhaps the rest of his life).

Monica became a lifelong friend of both myself and Madge and over the years, she would often drive up to Derbyshire in her campervan, park in the yard and keep an eye on things at home when I was away.

Monica, we owe you a lot.

WISHEE WASHEE, YOU'RE UNDER ARREST!

IT had been a hard day, two shows at the Thameside Theatre, Ashton Under Lyme, Greater Manchester. The pantomime was Aladdin and I was playing, as usual, the village 'loon', known in this panto as 'Wishee Washee'.

I was starving and, after the evening show, made my lone way to an excellent Greek restaurant. As I entered, I espied three members of the cast, all female. I'll give you their 'panto' names: there was 'The Slave of the Ring', 'So Shy' (the handmaiden), and Aladdin herself (i.e., a girl playing a male part).

They invited me over and we enjoyed a pleasant meal.

Towards the end, I was coming back from the toilet when I thought, why not treat the girls? So, there and then, without returning to the table and without the girl's knowledge, I paid the bill.

As he was giving me a receipt, I had another thought. I asked the manager if he would deliver to the table a facsimile of the bill I had paid but with the prices grossly inflated. He smiled and set to work.

Five minutes later, I saw him approaching the table and promptly engaged in earnest conversation with the lady seated opposite me. The bill was slid under the nose of the girl seated on my left, who glanced at it, gave a sharp intake of breath, and then said: "Oh my God, what?"

"What's the matter?" she was asked.

I looked at her; the blood had drained from her face.

"Look at these prices," she croaked, passing me the bill with a shaking hand. I looked at the document; it was a masterpiece.

The manager, who incidentally bore a marked resemblance to the master of horror movies, Vincent Price, had done a magnificent job. He had meticulously entered every item of food we had eaten, but had increased the cost considerably.

For instance: 1 chicken soup, £10.25. and 1 bread roll, £2.50.

The end result was that, on paper, we were each being asked to fork out over £50. (Bear in mind that this was many years ago, and the girls in question were only earning the equity minimum, about £150 a week).

They swallowed it hook, line and sinker and began to panic.

"Leave it to me, ladies," I announced, rising to my feet, "I'll have a word."

I made my way over to the manager, still within earshot of my fellow diners. I noticed that he had been joined by the rest of the staff, who didn't want to miss the fun.

They were a motley crew, two of the chefs were, to put it mildly, very heavily built (when did you last see a thin chef?) and wearing their kitchen whites, complete with hats. One of them looked a bit like Charles Bronson would look if he'd really let himself go, and I knew it was a wind-up.

I addressed Vincent Price. "We will not pay this bill," I said loudly and firmly.

"Why not?"

"It's too much."

"Too much, too much? You theatre people are all the same, you come in here and eat our food and now you refuse to pay. You will pay," (he paused for effect) "or else."

I heard a faint moan from the table behind.

"Don't threaten me," I roared.

Oh boy, I was enjoying this and what about Vincent, was he good or what?

"Listen to me, it's after midnight."

"So what?" I asked.

"Well sir, after midnight we can charge what we like."

Genius, I thought, the man's a bloody genius.

Now it was my turn: "That's it, I'm off. I refuse to pay this exorbitant amount."

With that, I flounced out through the door, leaving the girls to their fate.

This is where, once more, the mischief angels were doing their work. For there, outside the front door, was parked a Panda car containing two of Lancashire's finest. I approached the car and was recognised.

"Good evening, chaps."

"Good morning, you mean."

"Do you fancy a wind-up, fellas?"

"Try us."

I explained my plan, they agreed to participate and a few seconds later, I re-entered, followed by the two PC's.

We acted out a scene for the benefit of the girls: the argument became heated, insults were flung back and forth.

Finally, I was asked: "Will you pay this bill or not?"

"Never," I replied.

"Then you're nicked!"

And that was it, arm up me back and frogmarched out of the door.

As I was being hustled out, I yelled to the girls: "Phone David Lee (the panto's producer), and tell him I won't be appearing tomorrow, I'll rot in jail before I pay that bill."

So there I was, in the back of the police car and off, once around the block for effect.

"Thanks, fellers."

"You're welcome, Bern, it makes a pleasant change from arresting drunks."

I gave the girls a few minutes more as they tried unsuccessfully to negotiate a discount, unaware that the bill was made up and the meal had been paid for.

Then I re-entered and revealed it had all been a glorious wind-up.

Free drinks all around – and threats of retribution from the ladies!

THE DUSTY BIN JAPE

How Dusty Bin was rescued from a fate worse than death
(or spending the rest of his life with Hilary O'Neil)

During the eighties, one of the most popular TV quiz shows was called '321'. The host, Ted Rogers, had a sidekick, a 3ft-high, self-propelled, radio-controlled dustbin called 'Dusty Bin', which was an iconic figure, beautifully sculpted and familiar to the whole nation.

At the end of each show, the contestants, members of the public, were each given a small ceramic replica of 'Dusty' as a memento of their involvement. I have to stress that this figurine was very valuable and probably worth a couple of hundred pounds, even back then.

On the night in question, I was one of several actors and comedians who had been involved in one of the sketches, which were an integral part of the programme.

It was decided that we would 'wind-up' the comedienne and impressionist Hilary O'Neil by telling her that we had all been given a 'Dusty Bin' replica. To this end, we borrowed one from the security guard in the Yorkshire TV foyer (who made us swear that we would return it quickly as there was only a specific number to be given to the contestants later).

So, over around fifteen minutes, five or six of us paraded past Hilary, holding the treasured object (transferring it quietly to the next collaborator), convincing Hilary that we had all been given one and commiserating with her that she had been left out.

She swallowed it hook, line and sinker and got very, very upset. Realising that the prank had worked, we returned 'Dusty' to the relieved guard.

We were all going back to the Queen's Hotel for a late-night drink and I was giving Hilary a lift. As we were pulling away from the studio, she was still going on about how unfair it was that she had been overlooked,

"Where's your 'Dusty Bin'?" she asked.

"In the boot", I lied.

"That's it, stop the car."

She leapt out and stormed off into the reception area.

A couple of minutes later, she jumped back into the car, holding a small cardboard box.

"What you got there, Hils?"

"What do you think? I've got me 'Dusty Bin' haven't I? They're not treating me like that."

"So what did you do?"

"I went straight up to the security man who had all the boxes and told him straight, I said I'm Hilary O'Neil and I've been on the show same as the rest of them, they've all got one, so I'm having mine, and I just picked the box up and walked out."

This placed me in something of a quandary. She was carrying an empty box and she had 'boomeranged' the gag back on us, in which case, good for her, and we had been outsmarted; or, she actually had the 'Dusty Bin', in effect, she had stolen it and the fan was about to be hit by the proverbial.

I had to find out…was the box empty or not?

"Let's have a look."

"Why?"

"To see if it's the same as mine."

"Of course it's the same as yours. They're all the same, aren't they?"

This went on for ten minutes, she refusing to open the box and me being more and more convinced that it was empty.

Until finally, as we reached the hotel,

"OK, if it makes you happy."

Here it comes, lid up, rustling of straw for effect and surely I would hear, "Got you back, didn't I?"

But no. Out of the box came the one and only 'Dusty Bin'.

She really had (kind of) stolen it.

So now what was I gonna do? And what about that poor security guard that we had landed in it?

Hilary went up to her room to drop off her bags and freshen up and I hurried to the bar to regale my fellow conspirators with the news.

There was only one thing we could do and that was to steal it back from Hilary's room and return it, but how?

When Hilary came down, several of us were seated around a large table. She sat down and put her bag down under her chair, and I could see her room key lying on the top of her bag. A few minutes later, I stood up 'to go home', suffering cries of 'party pooper' from Hilary and having said exaggerated goodnights to everyone, went out of her eyeline and was able to crawl back on my hands and knees, reach under her chair and get the room key.

Everybody except Hilary could see me. My abiding memory of this manoeuvre was the reaction of the comedian, Alan Stewart. He was laughing hysterically and Hilary couldn't understand why.

I raced upstairs to her room, found the box, raced downstairs with it, crawled back, and replaced the key in the handbag (Alan was now in spasm and could have easily expired!)

I crawled out of the room, got into my car and, five minutes later, reunited 'Dusty' with a relieved security guard. Shortly afterwards, I strolled back into the hotel lounge and re-joined the party.

"I thought you'd gone home," said Hilary.

"Changed my mind."

And that was that, really. Later threats from Hilary to

get even never really materialised (not yet, anyway). It goes to show how things can so easily get out of hand once you let the 'mischief fairy' loose.

THE WALDORF HOTEL, RUSS ABBOTT AND A NERVOUS HALL PORTER

Clambering out of the limo provided by London Weekend Television one night, I had my hands full. There was my suitcase, my holdall, and an enormous white canvas sack containing the ostrich (or dodo/emu/chicken/duck as some called it).

As I struggled out of the car, who should be alighting from another LWT limo but superstar and all-round good egg, Russ Abbott.

"Bernie, don't struggle, I'll get the lads to help you."

On his bidding, one of the 'lads' bounded down the steps. This particular lad was a middle-aged, small in stature, and I mused, not strong enough to be carrying the dodo/chicken/duck (call it what you like) up a flight of stairs.

"Good evening, Mr Abbott, how lovely to see you." (This is how you're treated when you're a superstar).

"Hello, Joseph, this is my friend, Mr Bernie Clifton."

"Ah, Mr Clifton," (his Waldorf training prevented him from asking 'who?').

"Let me take the big one."

Big mistake: the 'big one' was a lot bigger than he was and, what's more, I had a thing about other people carrying it.

So I picked it up myself and we three entered the hotel, Russ in the lead (although a real good egg, you can't expect a superstar to stoop to carrying other people's luggage), I was a brave second, and Joseph came third, carrying the rest of my luggage.

Once in the hotel, Russ was greeted effusively by the staff, I, carrying the 'big one', was given some funny looks and Joseph was completely ignored.

It was at this point that I had to change hands, transferring the sack to my other side. In doing so, one of the false legs popped out of the bottom of the sack, giving the impression that there was a human inside.

Suddenly Russ was ignored, and I claimed centre stage.

In the midst of the hilarity that occurs during an incident like this, Russ invited me up to his penthouse suite for a coffee. It was agreed that Joseph would take the rest of my luggage up to my room, but I refused to part company with the ostrich (insecure, aren't I?).

So, Russ and I made our way to the lift, he still unencumbered by luggage and me carrying a large white sack with, apparently, a man inside it.

Once inside his suite, Russ and I chewed the fat and put the world to rights and then it was time for bed – or it should have been until Russ suggested getting Joseph to come up and carry the ostrich down to my room which is when I said: "Why don't I take the ostrich out of the sack, hide it in the bathroom and get into the sack myself with my legs sticking out as if they were the false ones."

And so, 15 minutes later, in came an unsuspecting Joseph,

"There it is, mate," said Russ, indicating the sack.

Now bear in mind Joseph had seen me carry the sack single-handed from the car to the lift earlier and therefore had every reason to believe he could do the same.

He bent over the bag, put his arms around my unseen waist and tried to lift me, without success.

He dropped to one knee and again tried, but no way! Then he started to freak out as he tried and failed for the third time to move me. During this final attempt, I was being grabbed in places I'd rather not mention.

"I don't like this, Mr Abbott, I don't like it."

No reply from Russ, who was blowing his nose loudly.

"I don't like this, Mr Abbott, it feels like a body."

Upon which he left the room at a fair rate of knots, saying: "I'm going for the manager".

As the door closed behind him, Russ helped me out of the bag, and within a minute, we had the ostrich back inside it and laid it out just where Joseph had last seen it.

I just had time to dive into the bathroom when the manager came in, followed by our Joe.

"Sorry about this, Mr Abbott, but he insisted I came up, he keeps going on about there being a body in the bag."

As he said this, he swooped on the bag and picked it up with one hand.

"Look, Joseph, it's just that flamin' ostrich, that's all. Come on, let's deliver it to Mr Clifton's room."

And with that, they were gone...end of story. You might think it was a cruel prank to play on the hapless Joseph, and I agree. That's the way it turned out, but I promise it's not what I intended. Mostly, the pranks are harmless...honest!

CHAPTER 16
HAVE TROMBONE, SHOULDN'T TRAVEL

AROUND 2005, I had my own afternoon show on Radio Sheffield.

Someone had dropped out; there was a reshuffle going on and, for me, it was 'right place, right time'.

I loved the job, meeting a variety of guests both live in the studio and on the phone and especially enjoyed the challenge of 'driving' the desk, watching the time, then fading the music in and out and winding down to finish right on the button for the hourly news.

I always kept my trombone in the studio. I couldn't play it (still can't, never will), but it had great comedy value in introducing items.

John Hemmingham came on the show one day. John runs the 'England Band', they are the official band that follow the England football team around the world to drum up support for the travelling fans.

He'd heard the trombone being used and asked me if I fancied joining the band.

I said: "No way, I can't play it. I just have it in the studio for a bit of fun".

He persisted, however, and in spite of my protestations, a few weeks later, I found myself in St James's Park, Newcastle, for a World Cup qualifier.

The band took up their position right at the back in the top tier of the main stand.

"I can't play it, John."

"You'll be fine, just stand next to me and follow."

The game started, I had a few skirmishes with the usual favourites, including the 'Great Escape' and 'God save the Queen', and came a bad second.

At half-time, John turned to me and said: "You're were right all along, Bern, you can't bloody play."

"I've been telling you that for the last three weeks."

"I thought you were kidding."

He added: "Don't worry, we'll get you some lessons".

The lessons were pretty basic: just learning the slide positions (from one to six) for each tune.

For instance, the slide positions for the 'Great Escape' are: 4 3 1 1 1 1 3 1 4, 3 3 1 2 1 2 4 1 4.

Next time you pick up a trombone, try it, see how you get on and imagine how you would have felt that night in Newcastle!

However, I persevered and during the World Cup qualifiers, I became a regular band member. I got cute, always standing next to big Ken, the euphonium player, as he was so loud that nobody could hear me anyway and as England progressed towards the finals, I thought, why not, and booked my tickets for the World Cup finals in Germany in 2006.

This part of my life is so bizarre: I'm in a band carrying a trombone I can't play.

To paraphrase Eric Morecambe... "He's playing (almost) all of the right notes (occasionally), and most certainly never, ever, in the right order".

As time wore on, the band travelled extensively following the national team and I was always there. Yes, I'm in a band and living the dream.

Moscow, Oslo, Copenhagen, Kyiv, Montenegro, Belarus, Trinidad: all of these places (and many, many more) have suffered from my lack of musical talent.

The band then became the official band of the British Ladies Hockey team, which meant a trip to Beijing for the Olympics in 2008. (If I wasn't writing, this knowing it to be true, I wouldn't believe it, so I'm not blaming you if you don't).

A man is in a band, he's travelling to the four corners of the earth, he's carrying a trombone, but he can't play it. You couldn't make it up!

Even better, the boxer Ricky Hatton had enrolled the band to follow him to Las Vegas, where they would become the 'Hatton Band'.

For me, though, there was a problem. Already struggling with the 'Great Escape' and the National Anthem, I was given an ultimatum: to make Vegas, I would have to extend my repertoire (Ooh Matron!).

Ricky Hatton had his own anthem, namely the Manchester City fan's favourite song, 'Blue Moon'. I had to learn it or risk missing the trip.

Forget 4 3 1 1 1 13 1 4, etc.; a whole new set of numbers beckoned, hence 'Blue Moon' was 3 3 3 1 3 1 1 3 3.

The only way I could remember these numbers was to write them on the back of the bell of the trombone, so I could read them while playing (and marching).

I was doing okay, I thought. Then on the afternoon of

the big fight, we assembled on the concourse of the Thomas Mack Stadium to entertain the crowd.

I say 'crowd', but I was in for a shock. The concourse ran around the entire indoor perimeter of the stadium, and although it was hours before the fight would start, it was packed with Hatton fans (the man had such a huge following).

Thousands, predominately male, had travelled from the UK to support their hero.

The band's line-up was three trumpets, two euphoniums, a drummer and an older guy 'playing' a trombone.

The idea was we would start playing, then march around, lapping the stadium until we could march no more.

I'd never been to a big fight before, and I'd describe the atmosphere as 'feral'. The fans were more than boisterous, boosted by their considerable consumption of alcohol.

They were ready for action and we were the catalyst for them to vent their emotions.

To a huge roar, we started our parade, round and round we went, and the noise from the crowd was incredible. We were two abreast, running the gauntlet between them as they roared their support in our faces.

I was just about handling the atmosphere but having trouble with 'Blue Moon'. It didn't sound right, even to my untrained ear. I played it again and again and thought perhaps I'd pitched it too high and I was in a different key to the rest. I just knew it was WRONG.

I had no option but to battle on: 3 3 3 1 3 1 1 3 1.

After about ten minutes, we came to a halt and shouldered our instruments to tremendous applause.

I turned to Big Ken, my euphonium-wielding

neighbour: "Sorry Ken, I just couldn't get the hang of that Blue Moon".

"Blue Moon?", he replied incredulously. "We weren't playing Blue Moon. We were playing, 'Walking in a Hatton Wonderland'".

I never lived it down, although the lads had to admit the two songs were similar.

The fight itself (which Ricky won) was less demanding of my abilities, we just 'chipped in' between rounds.

My very first Vegas experience was memorable, not only for my flawed trombone technique but for the journey home. We shuffled out of Gatwick Airport after a long overnight flight and, for some reason, I was travelling home alone.

The train north was my only option and would be difficult because of my luggage. I'd taken the ostrich over there (don't ask), which was contained in a large, round bass drum case; the trombone was in its own rigid flight case and I had my own large case and a small holdall.

I got as far as the station with all the above-mentioned items on the airport trolley, manhandled them down a flight of stairs to the scheduled platform, only to be told there was a change of platform, which involved me lugging my stuff up and then down two flights of stairs.

I made it on the train to Bedford, where I'd have to change to continue northward. On board, I was advised by the ticket collector (in the words of the song), "there may be trouble ahead".

The north of England had suffered extensive flooding overnight and rail travel was affected, but all I could do was plough on and hope for the best.

On reaching Bedford, I had well over an hour to wait and needed food. Balancing my stuff precariously on a trolley and with the help of both the lifts, I went up one level, across the footbridge and down the other side to where the cafe was located.

There was no room to enter, laden with luggage, so I left it outside the door where I could just, and only just, keep an eye on it.

Exhausted, I must have dozed off and awoke, realising I had only ten minutes to catch my connection. I went outside and found, to my horror, the trolley had disappeared.

I shouted at a passing employee, explaining that my trolley had been stolen. He had a muffled conversation on his intercom and then told me it hadn't been stolen, but because of security reasons, it had been taken to the manager's office on the central platform.

"WHY?"

"Security, unattended luggage."

"What's the point of putting it in the manager's office then?" I raged. "Doesn't it count if it explodes while he's sitting on it?"

I'd gone berserk, lost it completely.

I was at the eastern side of the station. My train was due any minute on the western side of the station and my luggage was in an office in the middle.

I raced up the stairs, across the footbridge and down the other side, recovered my trolley and, as I headed for the stairs, saw my train approaching, two sets of tracks away from where I was.

With the help of a hapless employee and a sudden surge of superhuman strength, I started to manhandle my belongings up the stairs, but thought I'd never make it.

Then something happened to me which I've never

experienced before or since: I turned into a monster, the kind of creature I would run a mile to avoid.

I became a kind of Basil Fawlty character. I rounded on the handful of people unfortunate enough to be in the vicinity and, purple-faced, bellowed...

"HELP ME, FOR GOD'S SAKE, HELP ME, DON'T JUST STAND THERE GAWPING, HELP ME!"

And they did! They were shocked into action and became my saviours – total strangers, all of them – grabbing my cases, running up the stairs, across the footbridge and down the other side.

Within a minute, together with all my stuff, I was on the train.

What had happened to me? In my desperation, an unrecognisable alter ego had emerged. (Perhaps we all have one buried somewhere, but it needs a series of events to surface).

A good or a bad thing: I've no idea.

On that day, I'd been without sleep, was jet lagged and carrying an impossible amount of luggage. I stood trembling as the carriage door closed in my face cutting short my pathetic thank yous.

I wonder how many times would the story be told over dinner that evening: "There was this lunatic at the station today with all this luggage. He had a big drum and a trumpet, I think; perhaps he was some kind of one-man band. Anyway, he seemed sort of deranged, so I thought it best to help him. Thankfully, I got him on his train and he seemed to calm down. I wonder where he is now?"

As to that question, read on: I had to stand all the way north from Bedford, which was bad enough, but things were to get much worse as the tannoy burbled,

"Ladies and gentlemen, owing to the track being

flooded north of the city, this train will terminate at Derby and a replacement bus service will be supplied to take passengers onwards to Chesterfield and Sheffield. I repeat, this train will terminate at Derby."

Oh, what a mess, but there was nothing for it but to plough on. Half an hour later, having found a trolley, I was in a queue of some two hundred people outside Derby Station, with the situation being controlled by a lady carrying a small loudspeaker.

We had about ten minutes of 'information' being relayed as to the arrival time of our bus' convoy'.

I was slumped over my trolley as she came down the queue and, as she passed within earshot, I heard her mutter to her colleague: "Imagine what they'll do when they find out there are no buses either".

I raised my head in alarm and, as I did, so saw beyond the front of the queue, perhaps 60 or 70 yards away, an oasis in the desert: it had a sign above the entrance, 'STATION HOTEL'.

To my rheumy eye, it read 'LAST CHANCE SALOON'.

I slowly moved my trolley sideways and calmly, so as not to cause alarm, walked past the front of the queue towards the hotel.

In spite of the load I was pushing, my pace quickened as I heard behind me, in magnified Derbyshire vowels: "LADIES AND GENTLEMEN, I'M SORRY TO HAVE TO TELL YOU..." (I had now broken into what could almost be described as a trot).

"THAT BECAUSE OF MAJOR ROAD FLOODING, NORTH OF DERBY..." (I broke into a canter).

"THE REPLACEMENT BUS SERVICE HAS BEEN CANC..." (I broke into a gallop).

I could hear the hoofs thundering behind me, closer

and closer as I reached the finishing line; I threw caution to the winds as I felt the hot breath of my pursuers on my neck. Throwing my burden aside, leaving the trolley and its contents upended on the pavement, I burst through the doors, hurled myself at the startled receptionist and croaked: "A ROOM FOR TONIGHT, PLEASE".

By this time, the mob were right behind me, behaving in a most agitated fashion.

"Oh you're lucky, sir; we have just the one room left."

The hate from behind me was palpable and ignored.

"I'll take it."

My fistful of fivers, US Dollars, even the odd one-armed bandit token landed on her desk.

I waited until I had my receipt and room key before I ventured outside to retrieve my luggage. There I found disconsolate groups of strangers making plans to either look for a city-centre hotel or perhaps share a cab to venture north.

l decided no good would come of even minimum eye contact, so with my head down, I shuffled indoors, found my room and slept the clock round.

Not quite the end of the story, though. Because of the chaos the flooding had caused, I booked an extra night and, about midday the following day, set off for a walk into Derby. Passing the station, I asked what the chances were of further travel. Nil by rail, I was told, but there's a coach about to leave to try to make it by road.

It was leaving from the other side of the station, a hundred yards from where I was and three or four times that distance from the hotel.

I trotted over to the waiting coach and saw the driver, who confirmed his imminent departure.

I said: "Great, I'll go and get me bag, will you wait for me?"

He looked at his watch: "Don't be long," he said.

To help make sure he would wait, I bagged a seat by throwing my jacket over the nearest available (the coach was almost full). I then jogged off back into the station.

I put on the afterburners and sprinted to the hotel. I explained to reception my situation, and as they cancelled my 'second night', I' press ganged' the porter. Between us, we grabbed all my stuff from my room and staggered all the way across the station.

The whole exodus took slightly less than 15 minutes, which was an incredible feat, but my entrance to the coach was greeted by a sea of sullen faces as I'd kept them waiting (the 'jacket over the seat' ploy swung it, as they couldn't leave without me).

Later in the journey, my star would ascend, however. The main road into Chesterfield was blocked, but I navigated us via a circuitous route. The end of a memorable trip (for some of the wrong reasons).

I was to visit Vegas again, but I'll never, ever forget the first time.

LIFE'S NEVER DULL WITH MY LONG-TIME MANAGER

Michael Vine has been my manager for more than three decades; before then he was a busy, well-respected cabaret artiste and magician.

He has since managed a number of artistes, including Joe Pasquale, Hilary O'Neil and myself. Oh yes, and Derren Brown. Derren is the world-famous 'mentalist'. I say 'mentalist' because I can't think of a better way to describe what he does. If you haven't seen him yet, it's time you did, he'll blow your mind.

Back to Michael and his weird sense of humour. Back in the nineties, I was constantly 'on the road' as I had a big following (and an even bigger mortgage). Around this time, Michael took a call from a company enquiring, "would Bernie be available to star in a touring summer show taking in various holiday centres across the UK". (Worth noting: that contract would span almost six months, a huge body of work and a considerable boost to my income). Michael's reply: "Oh, I doubt Bernie would be interested, in fact, I think he's retired."

Clearly, that reply could have cost me dearly. He did manage to extricate himself later by saying to that company: "Tell you what, let me check, I'll get back to you".

I once stood with Michael in the iconic Windmill Theatre, watching Joe Pasquale on stage rehearsing for a TV show.

The show's producer came by, Michael introduced him to me and said to him: "Bernie would be great for this show. Would you consider booking him?".

The producer, slightly taken aback but not wanting to be rude, said: "Oh, yes, let me think about it".

Without missing a beat, Michael reached into his pocket and produced a roll of bank notes, probably a few hundred quid, which he attempted to thrust into the guy's jacket pocket whilst saying, "will this help to seal the deal?"

The producer nearly fainted, wrenching himself away. "No, please, that's not necessary," he said before fleeing the scene.

Strange behaviour, but I love Michael dearly. Life's never dull in his company.

THE 'VOICE' AUDITION 2015

Hilton Hotel, please, I told the driver as I lowered myself into my seat. For the umpteenth time, I looked at the form: your 'Voice' Audition is on June 11, 2015, at 3.40pm. Please be prompt.

As the taxi left Piccadilly Station in Manchester I couldn't help asking, 'Bernard, is this a good idea?'. Yes, almost half a century after that unnerving singing audition in London, I'd agreed to another.

What possessed me to embark on what could easily be another traumatic experience? Let's face it, during the last 46 years, I'd been around the block a few times. How many times had I been around the world, entertaining all nationalities on the QE2 and on many more of the great cruise liners. I'd always been in great demand for cabaret and pantomime and had hundreds of TV appearances to my credit, including the Royal Variety Show, where, remember, I was told I reduced the Queen to tears of laughter. So why the need for another singing audition?

Let me explain. Over the years I'd invariably sing during my act and always finished with a big ballad. It's what I was brought up on.

The reaction was always favourable and usually prompted the comment: "Why don't you sing more?". But I was always booked as a comedian, so that's what I did. The singing just had to take a back seat.

Deep down, though, I was frustrated that I'd never developed my singing talent and then one day...I'm a Patron of the DTA Theatre Academy in Chesterfield, and one day I mentioned this to the owner Geoff Cox.

He uttered one word, "Carly."

"Who?" I asked.

"Carly, she's a fantastic young soprano, she trained with us, and now she's studying at the Royal Northern College of Music in Manchester. She'll know someone who can help."

A few days later, I met Carly (Carly is now known as Carly Paoli and is a huge star). She'd agreed to help, but first she needed to hear me sing. So there we were in my kitchen, her mum and dad outside in the car while I sang for her. She was impressed, and promised to put a word in with her vocal coach at the college. Which is why I found myself face-to-face with the renowned tenor and vocal coach David Maxwell Anderson. I convinced him I was deadly serious, that I thought I had a voice that could be developed and, even though I was in my mid-seventies, my voice had hardly been used. I just needed the right training. He heard me sing and agreed to take me on.

The lessons were hard work. Trying to lose the bad habits accrued over the years and finding the physical strength required was difficult. But I persevered and, over the coming months, I could hear the improvement. This gave me the confidence to sing with the orchestra run by my friend Greg Francis. They were touring evenings of Viennese music and I leapt at the chance of performing the Richard Tauber classics such as 'My Heart and I' and 'Girls were made to Love and Kiss', songs that I wouldn't have dared attempt a few months earlier.

As time went by, and thanks to the excellent coaching I was receiving, my voice continued to improve, but I realised that apart from the occasional concerts with Greg's orchestra, I hadn't found a vehicle to show people what I could do. Then, whilst watching the 'Voice' on TV, I saw the invitation to audition for the next series.

I knew there were risks attached. I might end up with

egg on my face, but I also knew that if I didn't go for it, I might regret it for the rest of my life. The old adage came to mind: 'don't die wondering!'

As we pulled up outside the hotel, my heart sank as there were hundreds of young people queuing around the block, all of them aspiring singers. I had a choice: go back home or join the queue. I joined the queue.

Best thing I ever did. The audition process was long-winded and wasn't easy, but the 'Voice' staff were fantastic; we could not have had better support.

My blind audition was televised in January 2016.

I watched it, alone by choice, with mixed feelings. On the one hand, I thought I could have done a better job of the vocal and, naturally, I was disappointed that the chairs didn't turn for me. On the other hand, the response from the studio audience and the judges (especially Ricky Wilson) when my identity was revealed was fantastic.

I met the judges backstage after the show and it was hilarious; a series of selfies were taken and I left the building with a good feeling.

The feedback via social media has continued to be very, very positive and my original desire to let the world know that, as well as running around on the back of an ostrich, I also had a singing voice had been achieved. Where it goes from here, I've no idea, but I'm continuing to train and treating the 'project' as a work in progress.

And while we're about it, if you have a talent you've neglected – it doesn't have to be singing, it could be painting or writing or pottery or anything – why not give it a go? Then perhaps an adventure is just around the corner for you.

If I can do it, anyone can.

So endeth today's lesson.

DUBAI

I must tell you John Adam's (remember him from earlier?) Dubai Airport story.

A few years ago, I found myself in Dubai, not only with my family – David, Jodie and Elliot, who live there – but also with John and Sue Adams plus their friend Mary (fellow godparent to son Christopher).

Mary was, and still is, a flight manager with Virgin Atlantic, so is referred to by John as 'Virgin Mary'.

She had organised a trip to Dubai for us all with the bonus of a discount, thanks to her crew status.

Once we landed in Dubai, I headed off to stay with my kids while John, Sue and Mary went to their hotel. We met up several times during the holiday and had a great time.

At the end of the holiday, we met up at the airport for our return flight. After check-in, with time to spare (we thought), the girls headed for the 'Duty-Free' with John in tow, and I went for a solo wander.

Dubai is a huge airport and, some time later, I realised I was leaving it late, so headed in the general direction of our departure gate. On the way I passed passengers disappearing through a gate displaying 'San Francisco' as their destination. One of them had left a trolley, which I commandeered. It was small, with an extra basket at waist level, which is where I deposited my hand luggage. My bag was really too large for its 'perch' and obliterated my view of the rest of the trolley.

A short time later, I came across John, seated alongside the walkway, looking absolutely exhausted. He said: "Bernie, they've worn me out; it was either sit down or fall down."

"Well, it won't be long now John, I'll see you at the gate."

"Yes, I'm meeting the girls there but not before I've had a rest".

I left him and did a 'Duty-Free Shop' myself.

About fifty metres from our final gate was a passport checkpoint.

"I'm sorry, sir, no trolleys beyond his point."

No problem. I removed my bag from the top shelf, then my heart almost stopped. There on the bottom shelf of the trolley was a brown leather holdall I'd never seen before, the type of luggage you see aircrew carrying.

"Oh, my God," I cried as I realised what I'd done. Back at the San Francisco gate, I'd taken the trolley and put my bag on the top, not spotting that someone's bag was on the bottom shelf.

I gabbled an explanation to the check-in staff, and after a hurried chat in Arabic, the younger male picked up the holdall and sprinted off back in the direction of the 'San Fran' gate.

By this time, I was told that the final check-in was closing and I had better hurry. To add to my panic, in the distance I could see John, Sue and Mary waving frantically by the gate. I got there breathless.

John said: "Bernie, have you got my bag?"

"WHAT?"

"My bag."

"No John, why would I have your Bag?"

"I put it on the bottom of your trolley when you stopped for a chat earlier on."

"WHAT? I didn't know; I never saw you do that."

"Where is it?"

"On its way to San Francisco."

"WHAT?" (will everyone please stop shouting, "WHAT").

Yes, John had popped his holdall on my trolley without telling me or me noticing. Chaos ensued, intercoms were employed, the conversations in Arabic became even more heated and I would rather not know how we, the departing Brits, were being described.

In the middle of all this we were told, in no uncertain terms, to "get on the plane now or miss it".

We hurried on board under the baleful glare of the seething passengers who'd been waiting the arrival of the 'one or two missing passengers' with barely suppressed rage. Hey, we've all been there!

The check-in staff had managed to stop John's holdall boarding a flight to San Francisco and threw it on board our plane as the door was closing.

Just another day at the airport for John and me.

Thanks for staying with me on that diversion to Dubai!

CHAPTER 17
'LAST LAUGH IN VEGAS'

THE email to Michael Vine went something like this…"Hi Michael, I wonder if Bernie would be interested in the following. We're putting a show together for ITV, which involves taking several 'mature' comedians to Las Vegas. They'll live together for two weeks in the resort before performing 'live' in a prestigious theatre.

The artistes we are looking for are those who were iconic figures on TV during the Sixties and Seventies and we believe Bernie would fit the bill perfectly."

Would I be interested? You bet I would!

Within weeks, I was having lunch with the producers, which seemed to go very well, and I left ITV in Salford with high hopes.

The next few weeks dragged by with no way of knowing whether I was in the frame. I consoled myself by thinking that there weren't many of us 'icons' who were still around, sitting up and taking notice. Over a 50-year period, I knew and had worked with all the names that were being mentioned, but I couldn't be sure I'd make the final group.

I then got a call to tell me they'd like to know more about me, which meant filming me at home. So a few days later, there I was, sitting on my sofa in a house that had never been as tidy since 'Through the Keyhole' in 1992!

During the interview, the phone rang a couple of times, I told the camera crew to ignore it, but they suggested I answer it as part of their 'at home' footage.

They filmed me taking the call and, lo and behold, it was their executive producer, Sally. I assumed she was trying to contact the crew and offered to hand them the receiver, but she stopped me and said: "No, I'm ringing to tell you that you're going to Las Vegas".

Well, I have to say, I went a bit 'ga ga', and got quite emotional, as this was such a big deal.

Here I was, an 81-year-old 'turn' (that's 'veteran entertainer' to you), been round the block a few (dozen) times, thought I'd done it all, but here I was being given a chance to go out in a blaze of glory by appearing in the showbiz capital of the world.

The series title said it all, 'Last Laugh in Vegas'.

Of course, they had filmed the call, it was all on camera, and they'd it all worked out beforehand.

But what great news! Look out, Vegas, here I come!

GETTING READY FOR VEGAS

The next few months were really busy. Apart from my weekly Radio Sheffield show, I was doing a summer season (remember them?) at the Spa Theatre in Scarborough. The 'Last Laugh' producer, John Kaye

Cooper, came over and we tried to hammer out my Vegas stage act.

John has been there and done it, bought the T-shirt, etc. You name it, he's produced it; amongst the highlights on his CV were those lavish ITV weekend spectaculars in the Seventies and Eighties.

When it came to my' spot', time was a problem as we had to boil everything down to around six minutes: not easy, but it had to be done. So Michael suggested we got Alan Wightman on board. Based in South Wales, Alan is a gifted comedy writer, and between us we would come up with six minutes that would work.

Meanwhile, all the acts were called to our first 'meet' and rehearsal. The venue was a studio complex, part of a huge building in: well go on, guess where.

If you were putting a Las Vegas show together in the UK, there's only place to do it, and that's Wigan. That's right, Wigan!

Joking apart, Wigan was perfect, certainly for the northern-based acts and it was close to Manchester, where the production company was based.

Although I hadn't been told officially who our fellow artistes were, the Bush Telegraph had been busy, and I thought I knew.

We rolled up one at a time for our first get-together in this giant rehearsal room.

There we were (in no particular order): Cannon and Ball, Mick Miller, Jess Conrad, Anita Harris, Bobby Crush, Kenny Lynch and ME.

Hang on, I'm one short. How could I forget that one-woman tornado, the giggle machine, the one and only Sue Pollard!

We all knew each other, over five decades, we had all

worked together, and the day was a riot: the insults flew, we shared memories and everyone felt good about the adventure that lay ahead.

But there was more to come. We were yet to meet the man we would come to call 'Mr Vegas'.

We were gathered around the piano where we had been running through our stuff with the musical director Andy Street, another one of those people in our business who everyone had worked with over the years. He was now based in L A and had been recruited to take care of the musical side of the Vegas show.

Great move, that. Top man was our Andy and, as a fellow Brit, it all helped to reinforce our comfort zone.

I was beginning to realise more and more what a big deal this was for me. To perform in Vegas would be a dream come true, but having Andy flown over from Los Angeles (to Wigan) for a rehearsal proved that ITV was leaving nothing to chance.

However, I was about to be confronted by another scenario, the possibility that it could all go very, very wrong.

The director was filming our reaction as he said: "Time to meet a man who is known as 'Mr Vegas', a legendary performer on the strip for 30 years, your mentor and Las Vegas producer...Frank Marino."

There was a collective clang as our jaws dropped; we were face to face with someone who personified everything that Las Vegas was. From his designer shoes to his mane of shoulder-length hair, he really was 'Mr Vegas'.

Now we, as a group of 70 and 80-year-olds, were in reasonable nick, but here was someone who looked amazing. Thirty years on the strip...he looked 25!

Frank, no shrinking violet, was upfront about his

appearance. He freely admitted he'd had 'some work done' (look him up as he's chronicled his 'alterations' on Utube). It's the Vegas way. Milky white, perfectly (re)arranged teeth, wrinkle-free (as a baby's bum) cheeks, chiselled, slightly tilted nose, there's more than one cosmetic surgeon in the States grateful to Frank for putting their kids through college (his words, not mine!).

The thing about our Frank is that he's happy for everyone to know he's had work done; it's the way it is in his world.

During his speech, he held nothing back: "A Vegas audience can smell fear".

There was worse to come for me, though. We all had to run through our stuff in front of Frank and the crew. This is always difficult for any performer, to rehearse your act without an audience is never easy. However, as I waited my turn, I could hear that his comments were very positive to Cannon and Ball: "Great, don't change a thing, keep it exactly like that".

My turn. I half walked and talked through my ideas, my confidence sinking by the minute. When I'd finished, he took a deep breath, the eyes twinkled, the nose tilted skywards, the teeth flashed and in that husky Vegas voice, he uttered the immortal phrase that sent a dagger through my heart: "BERNIE, YOU'RE THE ONLY ONE I'M WORRIED ABOUT."

I laughed, oh how I laughed. "Join the club, Frank," I said, "I'm worried about me too."

This could turn out to be an absolute disaster. During my career I'd worked to Americans on cruise liners many times and my act had gone down well, but maybe Vegas was different.

My misgivings were tempered as we left the rehearsal

rooms, with the oft-repeated cherished phrase: "See you in Vegas".

Although Frank had tried to console me by saying we could work together to get things in shape, my confidence had been dented, and as I drove back to Derbyshire, I was not the happiest of bunnies.

Back to Mr Wightman. Together with Alan and Michael, I had what I thought was a pretty tight spot that would work. So, undeterred, we carried on honing and putting in lines and moves to make it 'copper-bottomed'.

Remember, I was coming at Las Vegas from a different angle from the rest of the show. My collection of props worked with UK audiences; it's what I was known for, it's what they expected, but that little voice kept nagging away, 'what if Vegas doesn't get it?'.

The weeks sped by. Never mind the material for my act, I was having lots of hassle with my visa application, including a last-minute dash to the US Embassy in London, during which there was a memorable moment with an official there.

The issue was that we might be taking work from American 'artistes' by appearing in their backyard.

I was sitting face to face with a nice young man with a laidback drawl. He asked: "Is there a possibility that a US performer could do what you do in the show?"

I reached into my folder and slid across the desk a 10x8 coloured photo of myself, sitting on an ostrich, jumping over a wall.

His face was a picture, and he looked at it incredulously: "THIS IS WHAT YOU DO?"

"Yes," I replied,

"REALLY?"

His voice was getting higher and higher with each

question, one more and the light fittings would start to splinter.

"Kinda weird," he said as he was calming down, "hey, leave it with me".

The photo must have done the trick because ten minutes later, I was out on the street with the news that the visa would be in the post.

A big thank you here to the girls in the production office, who were amazing. They were on my case every minute, and I'm sure I wasn't the only one jumping through hoops.

The day of departure approached, and packing wasn't easy for me with the number of props I was taking, and I had to be ultra-careful that nothing would be left behind, so out came the giant trunk that had been around the world with me many times over the decades.

I was packing my stage suits and began to think they were a bit 'sober'; nothing among them seemed to shout 'Viva, Las Vegas'. So I rang Neil Crosland of StageWear International. Over the years, Neil has dressed EVERY club act who ever trod a northern board. I told him where I was going and he sent me some pictures of jackets that might fit the bill. One, in particular, took my eye and the following day, after my Radio Sheffield 'liveish' show, I drove north to Goldthorpe, a small place (former pit village) near Barnsley and there, down a side street, is an unimposing building I call his 'Aladdin's Cave'. Photographs of every 'turn' you ever heard of (and lots more you never) adorn the walls – the decades easily spotted by the changing styles, both in lapel width and hair length. Oh, boy, what did we look like in the seventies!

Every time I go to Neil's, we spend hours cracking up

at the 'mullets', the 'sideboards', the giant dickie bows and frilly shirts.

Now to the 'Vegas' jacket, it was mainly turquoise but checked with various bright colours, and it felt just right. More to the point, it fitted, so I bought it there and then and, two hours later, it was in the trunk.

I arrived at the hotel at Heathrow a day earlier than the rest for what was to be an amazing experience.

I was picked up and taken with some of the crew to the other side of the airport, the side that the public would never normally get near. The security was multi-layered and time-consuming, but well worth it for what was to follow.

We were given access to a 747 in an empty hangar. The producers had decided that some 'in-flight' entertainment for the rest of the passengers on our flight would be a good thing and, with British Airway's co-operation, we did a recce of this magnificent flying machine.

I was having the time of my life and the journey hadn't even started. The next 24 hours went with a whirl and, following lots more filming as we arrived at the terminal, we eventually settled down, ready for take off.

After lunch was served mid-flight, the flight manager made an announcement to the effect that the cabin crew were introducing a new member of staff and would passengers please welcome, on his first day at work, 'A Man on an Ostrich'.

So there I was, loping up and down the aisles on a jumbo jet. What the foreign passengers made of it, I've no idea. I'd done a few strange things in my time, but this took the biscuit!

VEGAS, I'M HERE

We landed at the airport in Las Vegas and, if we didn't know it already, it became clear we were part of a major TV show. We were filmed every inch of the way, asked to go back and do things again and again. This was tiring, as none of us were spring chickens and we'd come off a long flight, but our adrenaline was high.

The banter between the 'turns' was brilliant. Remember, we'd kind of grown up in the business together over half a century, and the one thing we had in common was our 'pro' sense of humour, without which none of us would have survived thus far.

The fleet of cars that took us from the airport arrived at the gates of a large villa, and when I say 'large', I mean really huge.

It was in the Spanish style, similar, to my eyes perhaps, to the residence of a Hollywood superstar. We were filmed getting out of the cars (several times), which was wearing us out. It was late in the day, the adrenaline had dropped and the jet lag was kicking in. Let's just say that we were all ready for bed.

On a table in the hallway of this magnificent house was a large envelope. With the cameras rolling, it was opened, and inside was a card: "Welcome to Vegas. Now go find yourself a bedroom and get some rest".

Well, you know the age-old holiday ritual of 'first down gets a lounger by the pool'.

Tiredness was forgotten as we went up the stairs like rats up a drainpipe, determined to get the best room we could. All the bonhomie, the lifelong friendships, went out of the window.

I've never seen Jess Conrad move so fast. I'm no slouch,

but Jess was quicker.

He was upstairs on the landing before you could say "rocket-powered stairlift".

As I scurried along the upstairs landing, I could hear pandemonium coming from various bedrooms: "I'm having this one," "I was here first", and "I'm not sharing with anyone".

We had all suddenly changed. We were now nothing more than knackered old tourists who wanted the best bedroom and were prepared to fight to the death to get it.

As I retraced my steps, I passed JC (that's Jess) framed in the doorway of his chosen bedroom. He was a big man, and his body language said quite clearly: "Thou shall not pass".

It became clear that, although we were nine in number, there were only six bedrooms: and nine into six won't go. Downstairs in the kitchen, things became heated, and voices were raised as people expressed themselves in no uncertain terms.

There was a common theme along the lines of: "I didn't come all this way to share a room. I don't share when I'm on the road back home, and I'm not going to start now".

Then everything changed! Someone had wandered outside and discovered, a few yards away across the courtyard, a cottage, and guess what? It had four bedrooms, and they were ours! What a relief!

We hadn't been made aware of the extra bedrooms. Was this by accident or design?

They wouldn't have let us squabble the way we did, on camera, would they, just to inject some drama into the show? Well, if they did, it worked.

We were ready to drop. Whilst outside, there was a glorious Nevada sunset, but our bodies were telling us it was 4 o'clock in the morning. We'd been up around 20 hours and we were out before heads hit pillows.

The following morning, we all staggered down for a DIY breakfast in a huge ranch-style kitchen. It's funny how as individuals, we're so different at this time of day. You've known people all your lives, but you don't really know someone until you've lived with them.

Most performers are not 'morning people'. For years, their bodies have learned to peak in the evenings or late at night when it's 'showtime'.

Ask any of them how they feel when, during panto, they have to do a series of 10 am shows for schools. Then, having posed the question, get ready to duck!

"It's not normal to put your 'slap' on and perform at that time; it should be against the law," they'll rant and rail.

So, that first morning in the kitchen, the conversation was muted.

I'm a 'tea first man' as I need that cuppa in my hand before I can start to function. I wasn't alone. Most of us were pottering around quietly…but not all of us.

There was one exception. The door was flung open and in came 'Storm Pollard'. Sue starts every day at 100mph, and she's loud, very loud. I'm not sure of her decibel count, but it's up there with Formula One and the Red Arrows.

One thing about the 'Pollard' is that, when she's around, you're never more than a few seconds away from gales of laughter. Great fun to be around, but not for too long!

I remember her trip 'up north' to say goodbye to Paul Shane, who was tragically losing his battle with cancer. Sue breezed into the hospice, champagne in hand, for his farewell party. Paul loved it and was still talking about it until the day he passed away shortly afterwards.

But out in Las Vegas, we came up with a way of 'switching her off'. We invented an 'on/off' button, hidden between her shoulder blades, so when she went 'off on one', we'd sidle up, press the spot, and sportingly she'd freeze.

Then, Mick Miller, the 'comic's comic', asked me if I remembered the 'shoes' gag I played on him. It was back in the early eighties and we were working the Circus Tavern Nightclub in Essex. I was there early, as usual, to set my props when Mick arrived, hung up his suit and unzipped his case, removing a shoe box. He revealed the contents, a beautiful pair of two-tone, patent leather Cuban-heeled shoes.

Proudly he said: "Just got these in London, never seen anything like em." They were special. I had only ever seen a pair like them once before, exactly like them. Two years earlier, in London, and I'd bought them.

However, my pair were no longer in any way even similar. I'd badly scuffed one of the toecaps, which meant they were finished as stage wear. Following the scuffing, I'd taken to wearing them on a day-to-day basis; then, after wearing them around the farm and playing football with the kids, they were all scratched and muddy, pretty well bashed up.

Shame, that. The good news, though, was that they were outside in the back of my car.

When Mick went out to grab a sandwich, I got my old pair and swapped them with his. I wrapped them individually in tissue paper, exactly as Mick had his wrapped, and placed them back in his case.

Later on, those of us in on the joke sat around as Mick got ready to go on stage. He put on his dress shirt, bow tie, shiny mohair trousers and then unwrapped the shoes.

I'll never forget the look on his face as he took them out of the wrapping. He gazed at them in disbelief. That beautiful pair of unique stage shoes he'd wrapped up and put away a couple of hours ago were now unfit to put on just to take the dog out.

"What the?"

Just at that moment, I stood up and walked across the room, wearing his pair.

"Excuse me, Mick, I think you've got my shoes there."

Over thirty years later and he'd not forgotten. Everybody loves the Miller Man, placid to a fault, dry as a bone, with just a hint of a weary smile as he delivers gem after gem in his unique, deadpan Scouse style.

Before the Vegas show, I knew Kenny Lynch least of all but got to enjoy his approach to the whole experience, hearing his laidback gravel voice, constantly cutting through conversations with remarks like '"what am I doing here?" and "do I really need this?"

What a great way of dealing with the stress!

Kenny had us spellbound with his tales of where he'd been, what he'd done and the stars he's still on first-name terms with. He knows EVERYONE, and then to hear him sing, so cool.

Anita Harris is such an adorable lady, such a sweetie; what you see is what you get, not a bad word to say about anyone, under the cosh like the rest of us but always held it together in her serene style. Lovely Anita even shared some vocal technique advice with me during the build-up.

Bobby Crush reminded me of the trouble we got ourselves into back in 1979. We were in summer season at the Knightstone Theatre in Weston-super-Mare, and me and Bobby thought it would be funny if we put on some entertainment during the interval without telling anyone. We rehearsed it between ourselves.

On the fateful day, the curtains closed on the first half, and the audience left the auditorium and headed for the bar.

Three minutes later, hearing music and thinking the second half was starting, they hurried out of the bar without buying any drinks and sat down again. There we were on stage, me and Bobby, but not as ourselves. He was dressed up as a very old lady, and I was dressed like a very old gentleman. He (she) was on piano singing in falsetto, and I sang in the manner of a straight-laced baritone), the pair of us duetting with a medley of (wait for it), the 'Village People'.

'Bobby' hammered away on the upright piano: "IN THE NAVY," 'she' shrieked, "Y M C A", I bellowed.

It lasted three minutes and ended with the curtains being drawn to the sound from the audience of an excruciating silence.

They sat watching with mouths agape; they had no understanding of what they had just sat through.

They had paid good money to watch a family variety summer show and had seen...what?

The only certainty was that the bar interval takings were down by a substantial amount.

We got the biggest rollocking imaginable. There was talk of us having to reimburse them for the lost revenue but, fortunately, that wasn't enforced.

Needless to say, the bar at the Knightstone Theatre was out of bounds for some time.

Jess Conrad, at 80, is still a handsome man and if you want confirmation of that description, just ask him. Jess has the gift of still being able to sell himself as a superstar, but done with a nod, a wink and a flash of those pearly whites that says, "relax, I'm in on the joke, too, darlings". I saw him in an Aladdin panto playing the evil Abanazaar. In the middle of a heavy dramatic scene, Jess would produce a mirror from his waistband, gaze at himself adoringly and say: "You're much too beautiful to be evil". One of a kind, our JC!

As for Cannon and Ball, I have left them until last because they're 'bill toppers' (they weren't always though, read on). After serving their time in the northern clubs, Tommy and Bobby made it not just big, but proper BIG, becoming household names with the phrase "Rock on, Tommy," becoming part of the nation's vocabulary. Yes, this couple of welders from the north took the nation by storm.

I first met them in 1973. At the time, I was the compere at the Aquarius Night Club in Chesterfield. During the day, I worked in the office as the club booker. We'd heard about this double act who were making a name for themselves around the clubs, so I rang up and booked them for a week. Acting on the reports I'd heard, I took a chance and put them in as the headline act with three supporting acts…a proper variety bill.

The lads turned up for band call on Sunday afternoon, and when they saw the posters, they had what can be described as a 'squeaky bum' moment.

Cornering me, they said, "we can't top the bill; we're only a support act" (or words to that effect).

I placated them, reassuring them that they'd be fine and not to worry. As showtime arrived, though, they were still 'bricking it'.

I gave them a great build-up, on they came and, of course, they were brilliant and brought the house down. I've never let them forget our first meeting and take every opportunity of winding them up, reminding them that without me, they'd be nothing. I was the one who gave them their first break, took a chance and made them stars. It's worth it just to see the baleful look in Bobby's eyes as he decides on a way to get his revenge.

So there you have an insight into my relationship with Tommy and Bobby and perhaps an insight into the way we all interacted as a group. Okay, there were tensions from time to time as there would be in any large family, but I think there was an underlying mutual respect.

My overriding memory of those first few days in Vegas is a mixture of excitement, exhaustion, but most of all, hysteria. We were having fun, make no mistake. Here we were, elderly entertainers, obviously on the last leg of our respective careers, being given the chance of a 'lap of honour' which, let's face it, none of us thought we'd ever get.

Turning eighty and going on stage in Vegas for the first time? You couldn't write it!

Although our real reason for being there, our stage show, was looming, we were being kept busy with all kinds of activities, some strenuous, some bizarre, on a daily basis.

I'll mention one briefly. One day we were taken into the desert in our fleet of luxury people carriers. We stopped in the middle of nowhere when, out of the scrub, appeared a gang of 'gun toting' (love that phrase) bandits on horseback who, firing away, surrounded us and ordered us out of our vehicles. All carefully stage-managed for the cameras, of course, but very impressive nevertheless. Further adventures in the 100-degree heat awaited us.

Then there were the morning yoga classes...with GOATS! Only in Vegas!

We were being kept very busy; every day there would be an excursion (or two). The itinerary was full, we got tired in the heat, but this was a once-in-a-lifetime trip and we were determined to enjoy it.

The days flew by, and as we got into the show rehearsals, the clock ticked ever faster.

Once we'd seen the venue, our minds became really focused on why we were there, and our daily excursions became more of a distraction.

TODAY'S THE DAY

Up at the crack of...

The convoy arrived at the theatre.

They were always long days in Vegas, and this was no exception: band rehearsals, technical run, dress rehearsal, last-minute tweaks, and we were ready.

I was sharing a room with Bobby Crush and almost managed to flood the place by failing to turn off the tap in the shower room. Fortunately, there was a mountain of paper towels on top of the wardrobe, which I just threw onto the bathroom floor to avert a disaster.

ON STAGE IN VEGAS

I remember standing in the wings for my first Royal Variety Performance in front of the Queen, nervous as hell, and I'd muttered to myself, "just enjoy it".

Forty years later, there I was repeating the mantra...and I DID enjoy it.

Suffice to say I had a memorable evening.

You want an audience to love you, and the best way they can demonstrate that is to give you a standing ovation. For that to happen in Las Vegas was beyond my wildest. I'll never forget it if I live to be a hundred.

Like everyone involved, Frank Morino was very emotional backstage afterwards, it had been quite a journey for us all and he'd been on board all the way.

And it was over, we'd done it: we'd had our 'Last Laugh in Vegas'. I loved the whole experience.

The production teams, both UK and American, deserve a huge thank you. I know they put us through more than a few hoops, but they were always there for us, nurturing and cajoling us 'old uns' so we made it past the post.

The series did me no harm at all; in fact, it gave me a springboard. With major input from my good friend, the multi-talented Neil Makin (I can see him blushing), we've put together a stage show billed as 'From Crackerjack to a Standing Ovation in Las Vegas'.

I'm on stage for an hour and a half telling it as it is (and was). I've got a hundred images to back up the stories, plus video clips as well as backing tracks to do some 'proper' singing (which is where I bring in Pius Hume). Over the years, I kept hearing about this singing teacher called Pius (there's a name you can't forget).

Eventually, I tracked him down and thanks to Pius, at the tender age of 82, I embarked on a singing career.

I've had some amazing coaching in my time, but Pius seems to have revealed even more of the hidden voice I always thought was there.

He said something interesting recently when I was thanking him for my progress.

I said: " How I wish I'd met you ten years earlier."

His reply: "I'm so glad you didn't. Ten years ago, I didn't know half of what I know now."

So we are all on a learning curve. I was having so much

fun singing…then I was back in pantomime.

It was December 2018, and I played Baron Hardup in Cinderella at the New Theatre, Hull, alongside the lovely Anita Dobson. It went so well, the whole production was transferred to the Derngate Royal Theatre in Northampton for the 2019 panto season. We opened to rave reviews, and it really was a terrific show with an amazingly talented cast. To say I enjoyed the panto is an understatement.

NOW I'VE FINISHED (OR THOUGHT I'D HAD)

I began working on this book several years ago. It's been a real labour of love and a test of my discipline to keep my head down and write (I've often failed!). It could easily have been a book full of japes and practical jokes, as they played a huge part in my life, but hopefully, I've kept them down to a few.

Early on, I made an important decision: the book was never going to be 'warts 'n all'. Some of my own personal foibles (and tragedies) are included, but my family and close friends are living their own lives and have a right to privacy. I won't disrespect that, as it's not my style. If you're looking for the 'Full Monty', this ain't for you. However, I have tried to show what took that little lad with clogs on his feet from a back street in St Helens, to a standing ovation in Las Vegas. It was down to humour, bloody-mindedness, a great work ethic, plus plenty of luck along the way. Mistakes, I've made many! But, I got through somehow.

What a journey…

Yours, **Bernard Quinn**, failed student, plumber, boy singer
and Ostrich Jockey (retired).

But, before I go, I couldn't leave without mentioning the 'Squire of Notty Ash', the late, great, Ken Dodd. Ken was not only a close friend, but an inspiration to all of us. Thank you, Ken. I'll leave you with this...

We all went off to Liverpool, to say goodbye
*   to Ken*
If we live to be a hundred, we won't see his like
*   again.*
The church was overflowing, no room for
*   everybody*
Thousands came from miles around to say
*   goodbye to Doddy.*
That Liverpool cathedral, was packed up to the
*   rafters*
To say goodbye to a special guy who filled our
*   world with laughter.*
Ken would have liked the service, as we watched
*   the hours pass.*
They had to have an interval to squeeze in a
*   midnight mass.*
The Jam Butty Mine closed early, as a tribute to
*   the boss*
The diddy men in mourning, dealing with their
*   loss.*
Plus people from St Helens, Ken called us
*   woolybacks*
We'll be thinking of you Doddy every time we pay
*   our tax*
Now just inside those pearly gates, he's putting
*   on a show*
They're looking at their watches, but they won't
*   want to go*

St. Peter says, "Is Ken still on? It's been a year or
   three.
He's brought a whole new meaning to the word
   'eternity' "
So a fond farewell to you Ken Dodd, you're
   missed for evermore
You're up there with your heroes, all those who've
   gone before,
Arthur Askey, Tommy Cooper, Les Dawson,
   Morecambe and Wise,
But you'll always be the number one, to you, Sir
   Ken...tatty bye!

ACKNOWLEDGMENTS

And now the end is near, and so I face the final (pages), I'm thanking everyone who's made this book possible.

There's my publisher (get me, 'my publisher'). It would never have happened without Robert's patience during these last few months. It's taken years to get this far, and even as we're heading for the printers, I'm still coming up with memories and anecdotes I'd like to include, but I can't.

We've already run over our intended release date by several weeks and now it's time to close the project. I've passed my 87th Birthday, so it's unlikely I'll be writing another. This is it! There are far too many people out there to thank personally, far too many to mention here. So, I'll concentrate on my immediate family.

I told you earlier of a comedian's wife once saying, "It's alright for you lot, what about us? We only get what's left." She was perhaps speaking for the families of entertainers everywhere.

On the subject of families, my wife Madge sadly passed away in 2000 after suffering from dementia for several years, and then tragically, my eldest son Stephen died in January 2023 with complications following a short illness.

These tragedies have naturally taken their toll, but I'm very lucky to have the constant love and support from my family through it all. This has made it possible for me to continue working and I've been able, (as me Dad said) to "Keep on, Keeping on".